OSC IB STUDY & REVISION GUIDES

FOR THE INTERNATIONAL BACCALAUREATE DIPLOMA PROGRAMME

History

Paper 2: Authoritarian States
Germany 1918–1945

SL & HL

FSC

Joe Gauci

OSC IB Study and Revision Guides
Published by OSC Publishing,
Belsyre Court, 57 Woodstock Road,
Oxford OX2 6HJ, UK

History
Paper 2: Authoritarian States Germany 1918–1945
SL & HL
© 2017 Joe Gauci
9781910689233
233.02

The material in this Study and Revision Guide has been developed independently of the International Baccalaureate Organisation. OSC IB Study and Revision Guides are available in most major IB subject areas. Full details of all our current titles, prices and sample pages as well as future releases are available on our website.

How to order

Orders can be made via the website, e-mail, fax, phone or mail;
contact numbers and addresses below.

OSC
Belsyre Court, 57 Woodstock Road
Oxford OX2 6HJ, UK
T : +44 (0) 1865 512802
F : +44 (0) 1865 512335
E : osc@osc-ib.com
W: osc-ib.com

Printed and bound by CPI Group (UK) Ltd, Croydon CR0 4YY
www.cpibooks.co.uk

Preface

 I have taught History for the past thirty years in independent schools in the UK, including teaching the International Baccalaureate (IB) for twenty-three years at Malvern College, as well as teaching on OSC Spring revision courses and Summer schools for the past twenty years. I am never happier than when discussing approaches to key historical questions with students, exchanging ideas about different perspectives that can be taken on the past. So, working on this study guide has been a real pleasure, and I have tried to take approaches in writing it that my experience over the past thirty years has shown work best in preparing students to tackle essay questions.

I have always enjoyed writing history essays and helping students prepare for essay-based examination papers. For history students, generally essay-writing is the biggest challenge they will face. Writing a very good or excellent essay requires both a very secure understanding of a lot of historical information and a mastery of a range of essay-writing skills: interpreting the question; planning an effective approach to the question and creating a clear structure; writing an introduction that identifies the themes or factors the essay will explore and the thesis of the essay; developing a clear line of argument and keeping focussed on the title; selecting and deploying precisely an appropriate range of supporting evidence and, restating the main argument of the essay in order to provide a strong conclusion.

How to Use This Guide

In terms of technique, the guide starts with a section of advice on how to approach essay questions. In addition, I have provided practice essay questions, partially completed by me but with space for you to have a go too.

This guide contains detailed notes on the emergence and rule of Hitler's authoritarian state in Germany. There are 'Key Term' boxes throughout the guide, providing information relating to key terms and definitions which are important to know when studying Nazi Germany. There are also 'Key Historical Perspectives' sections, which explain important debates among historians about Nazi Germany.

What parts of the IB History syllabus is this guide useful for?

1. Primarily, this guide is intended to help Higher Level and Standard Level candidates who are studying Hitler's Germany as a case study for World History Topic 10: 'Authoritarian States (20th Century)', for Paper 2.

2. In addition, it will be of help to Higher Level candidates who are studying Weimar Germany and Hitler's Germany as part of Higher Level Option 4: History of Europe, Syllabus Section 14: European States in the Inter-War Years (1918–1939).

Contents

Advice on Tackling Paper 2

What do you need to know?

- The examination lasts one and a half hours.
- It is divided into twelve sections, each on a different world history topic.
- Topic 10 is 'Authoritarian States'.
- Two essay questions will be set on each topic, so there are twenty-four in total.
- Candidates have to answer two questions, each chosen from different topics.
- The maximum mark for each question is 15.
- For Higher Level candidates, Paper 2 is worth 25% of the total assessment.
- For Standard Level candidates, Paper 2 is worth 45% of the assessment.
- The questions will be open (you can use your own examples); they will not refer to either named states or leaders.
- The IB syllabus specifies that the following aspects of authoritarian states should be studied:
  - The emergence of authoritarian states
  - Consolidation and maintenace of power
  - Aims and results of policies.
- Some questions will demand discussion of states from more than one region (there are four world regions as defined in the International Baccalaureate Organization [IBO] handbook) and the IBO recommend that students study a minimum of three authoritarian states.

Advice on Tackling Essays

- You must spend a few minutes carefully looking at the paper and weighing up the choice of questions, before you make up your mind on which two questions to answer.

- Look very closely at the wording of the questions, making sure that you understand their implications and what you need to address in your answer.

- Pay particular attention to 'command' words such as: 'to what extent', 'examine', 'compare and contrast'. In the case of 'To what extent was any one authoritarian state you have studied a totalitarian state?' you must weigh up the ways in which it was and the ways in which the Nazi state was not totalitarian, reaching a conclusion about whether it was totally, largely, partly, or not at all, totalitarian. 'Compare and contrast the methods by which two leaders of authoritarian states came to power' would require you to examine the similarities and the differences between their methods. 'Examine' means identify and scrutinise, so 'examine the conditions which gave rise to an authoritarian state' would require you to identify the circumstances which made possible the Nazi Party's success, explaining which conditions (social, political, economic, military) benefited the Nazis and evaluating which were most important.

- Always plan your answer, spending at least two or three minutes doing this for each essay, if not longer (but no more than five to six).

- Give equal time to each essay you write. Do not be tempted to spend much longer on one at the expense of the other.

- Answer the question. Keep your approach analytical; do not drift into a description of events. Focus tightly on the question; do not deviate.

- Perhaps the best way of ensuring that each paragraph is linked to the title is to check that your first sentence (the 'key' sentence) is making a statement that directly answers the question.

- For each point that you make, provide an explanation of what light that point sheds on the question and why it is significant—you should also present evidence or a precise example to support it. So, the drill should be 'Statement, Explanation, Example'.

- Always write in complete sentences and be as clear as you can in your use of English. The clearer your English, the more effectively you will communicate your points to the examiner.

- Always write a proper introduction. This must identify the key issues raised by the question. You should also outline your thesis, the line of argument that your answer will take.

- Make sure that you leave time for a proper conclusion. The main purpose of this is to restate your key arguments.

- Do not feel that you have to pack your answer with references to differing schools of historical interpretation and named historians. You will get credit for such historiographical references, where used appropriately, but do not insert them just for the sake of displaying your knowledge if they do not contribute to answering the question.

- Whatever information you insert into your answer, whether in the form of a fact, a statistic or a quotation, do make sure that you explain its significance and how it answers the question. If you do that, your essay should remain focussed.

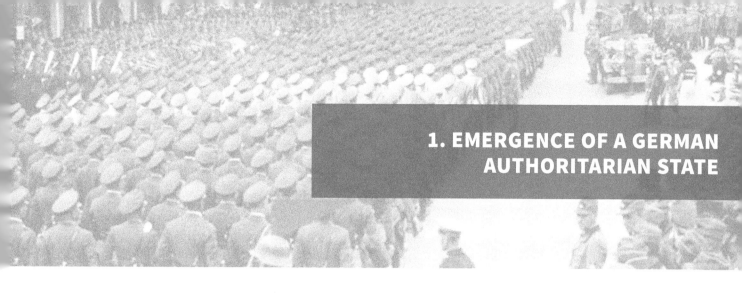

1. EMERGENCE OF A GERMAN AUTHORITARIAN STATE

TOPICS:
Long-term conditions
Short-term conditions
Methods

In using Germany as your case study for answering a question on the emergence of authoritarian states, it will be necessary to examine both the weaknesses of the **Weimar Republic** and the strengths of the Nazi Party.

1.1 Overview of Germany (1918–1933)

There is no doubt that the democratic republic set up in Germany at the end of the First World War faced serious problems from the start. The period up to 1923 saw a series of crises that threatened to overwhelm the Weimar Republic. However, under the guiding hand of Gustav Stresemann (briefly chancellor and then foreign minister), in the years 1924–1929, the Republic appeared to become more stable economically and politically. This recovery was cut short by the **Wall Street Crash** in October 1929, which led the USA to recall huge loans to Germany, resulting in the collapse of the German economy and large-scale unemployment.

Democratic government in Germany began to break down as no chancellor between 1930 and 1932 was able to construct a coalition government that commanded a majority in the **Reichstag**. Rising unemployment and weak government transformed the fortunes of the Nazi Party (founded in 1919). From a tiny extremist party with just 2% of the seats in the Reichstag in 1928, the Nazis became the largest party in Germany in 1932. In January 1933, the conservative president, Paul von Hindenburg, appointed Adolf Hitler chancellor in a cabinet containing just three Nazis. Hindenburg's assumption that he and his conservative allies would be able to control Hitler was quickly confounded. Within six months Hitler had created a single party dictatorship.

1.2 Background

Germany, as a single, unified state, was not created until 1871. Up until 1866 there had been thirty-nine separate states. One of the largest of these states, Prussia, proceeded to absorb the others by means of wars against Austria (1866) and France (1870–1871). In 1871 the German Empire was proclaimed. The new Germany, in spite of having an elected *Reichstag*, had an authoritarian system of government with power chiefly wielded by the **Kaiser.** Germany underwent rapid industrialisation, overtaking Britain as Europe's leading industrial country, and developed the most powerful army in Europe.

Kaiser Wilhelm II (1888–1918) pursued an aggressive foreign policy that played a major role in creating the tensions that sparked off the First World War in 1914. The German government had anticipated a short victorious war, defeating France and Russia by means of the Schlieffen Plan. However, the plan failed to deliver a quick victory and Germany, and its ally, Austria-Hungary, became locked into a long and costly war of attrition against the countries of the Triple Entente (Britain, France and Russia). In 1917 Germany decided to launch a campaign of unrestricted submarine warfare in an attempt to starve Britain into surrender. However, Britain hung on and the gamble backfired as it provoked the USA into declaring war on Germany. Germany's hopes of victory were not totally extinguished because in 1917 Russia dropped out of the war following two revolutions, the second of which brought Lenin's **Bolsheviks** to power. In spring 1918, the Germans launched a massive offensive against the French, British and Americans. After initially breaking through the Allies' lines and pushing them back towards Paris, the German attacks lost momentum and, from August, the Allies mounted a succession of powerful counter-attacks which drove the Germans back.

By September 1918, the German military leaders, Hindenburg and Ludendorff, accepted that Germany could no longer avoid defeat. In October, the *Kaiser* reluctantly agreed to begin ceasefire talks with the USA and at the same time appointed a cabinet drawn from leading figures in the *Reichstag*, with the **liberal** Prince Max of Baden as chancellor. Wilhelm II seemed to have hoped that this concession would enable him to preserve the monarchy in Germany and that it might incline the Allies to treat Germany more generously in the post-war peace negotiations. However, the *Kaiser's* government quickly began to lose control over the country as a wave of riots, strikes and mutinies broke out. Germany's soldiers, sailors and civilians were angry to find out that Germany was on the verge of defeat after four years of hardship, extreme shortages and two million soldiers killed. For a time, it looked as if Germany might follow Russia's recent example and undergo a violent revolution. In an attempt to contain the upheavals, Hindenburg and Prince Max told the *Kaiser* that he had to abdicate. On November 9th 1918 the *Kaiser* fled to Holland, and Germany was declared a republic. Two days later, the new socialist government, led by Friedrich Ebert, signed a ceasefire with the Allies, bringing the First World War to an end.

The new government announced that elections for a **Constituent National Assembly** would be held in January. In these elections, the main parties that supported democracy— the Social Democratic Party (SPD) [a moderate socialist party], the Democratic Party (DDP), and the **Centre Party (ZP)** [a party representing Germany's Catholics]—gained over 70% of the votes cast.

In February, the Constituent Assembly opened at Weimar (rather than in Berlin where violent disturbances had broken out) and Friedrich Ebert (SPD) was chosen as Germany's new president. Philipp Scheidemann (SPD) became Chancellor. The Independent **Socialists** (USPD) refused to join the government so Scheidemann formed a **coalition** with the ZP and the DDP. The Assembly voted in July to adopt the newly drafted constitution.

1.3 Long-Term Conditions That Gave Rise to an Authoritarian State

1.3.1 Weakness of Germany's Democratic Political System

It was to prove very difficult to establish a democratic system of government in Germany in the wake of military defeat and economic crisis.

What long-term problems faced the Weimar Republic?

- Without necessarily accepting that the Weimar Republic was doomed to fail from the start, it is clear that it faced serious problems in the years immediately after the First World War. Moreover, although the Republic survived the early crises and became more stable in the mid-1920s, these threats and early weaknesses did not disappear.
- The world economic crisis of 1929 plunged Germany into renewed crisis and the long-term weaknesses of the Republic were cruelly exposed, contributing to the collapse of democracy in 1933. Therefore, any assessment of the rise of a single party state in Germany must examine the long-term problems facing the Weimar Republic.

The Versailles Treaty (1919)

The new democratic government of Germany was obliged by the Allies to accept peace terms at Versailles in June 1919. Unfortunately for the Weimar Republic, many nationalists blamed the new Socialist government for agreeing to the Armistice (ceasefire) in November 1918, and the Versailles Treaty the following June, claiming that the German army could have fought on if it had not been stabbed in the back by cowardly, democratic politicians.

Although modern historians are divided about how hard these terms, particularly **reparations**, hit Germany, there is no doubt that they caused widespread resentment among Germans at the time.

> **Key Term**
>
> **Reparations:** financial compensation that Germany was obliged to pay its enemies in compensation for war damage and loss of life.

What aspects of the Versailles Treaty did Germans resent?

- The German government was unable to negotiate the terms of the treaty; Versailles was a *diktat* (dictated peace), which had to be accepted in full or war would resume.
- Germany lost about 13% of its European territory (plus all of its colonies). What was particularly criticised by Germans was the loss of land in the east; over two million Germans ended up living in the new Polish state or in Danzig, under League of Nations' control.
- The Allies were inconsistent in applying the principle of national self-determination; the Poles were united to create a new Poland and Slavs in the Balkans were united in the new state of Yugoslavia, but Germans living in the Sudetenland (part of the former Austro-Hungarian Empire) were placed under Czech rule and Germany was forbidden to unite with German-speaking Austria.
- The reparations imposed on their country; the final figure was fixed in 1921 at £6,600 million. The German government claimed that this would cripple Germany, a view shared by the British economist, John Maynard Keynes. However, some recent historians, such as Ruth Henig challenge this, arguing that the German government exaggerated the burden and that more damage was caused by the way in which Germany chose to pay it off (by increasing the supply of paper money).
- That Germany's armed forces were severely restricted; the army's size was fixed at 100,000; **conscription** was banned; Germany was not allowed submarines, an air force or tanks; the Rhineland was to be permanently demilitarized and, the German navy could only possess six warships.

Figure 1.1: American cartoon from New York World (1921) suggesting that reparations were an unreasonable burden on Germany.

> **Key Term**
>
> **Conscription:** compulsory military service.

Political opposition to the Weimar Republic

The Weimar Republic, so-called because the Constituent Assembly met in the town of Weimar, got off to an extremely difficult start and was dogged by crises over the next four years. There were extreme **right-wing** and **left-wing** movements in Germany that were opposed to democracy and were committed to overthrowing the Weimar Republic.

Threats from the Left

In January 1919, an extreme left-wing socialist movement known as the **Spartacists** set up the German Communist Party (KPD). The KPD rejected the new German Republic as insufficiently revolutionary. The KPD was committed to establishing a Bolshevik-style system of government in Germany, involving the confiscation of privately owned factories and land. Over the next four years the Communists organised a series of risings but none of them came close to overthrowing the Republic. From 1920 the KPD contested *Reichstag* elections and polled between 10 and 15% of the votes cast in the elections of 1928–1933. Their continuing hostility to the Republic did undermine its prospects of long-term survival, particularly as it meant that the Left was badly divided between the KPD and SPD who would not work together (except in the case of 1923 in a couple of states). This made it easier for Hitler to come to power in 1933.

1. The Spartacist Rising (January 1919)

In early January 1919, some of the Spartacists staged a rising in Berlin. This was bloodily put down by the *Freikorps*, bands of extreme right-wing ex-soldiers. The Spartacist leaders Karl Liebknecht and Rosa Luxemburg were murdered.

2. Communist Risings in the Ruhr (March 1920) and Munich (April 1920)

In March the Communists staged an uprising in the Ruhr, setting up a government at Essen and in April they briefly took over Munich. The *Reichswehr* (German Army) was prepared to intervene and bloodily restored order, killing hundreds of communists.

3. 'The German October' (1923)

The **KPD** organised street demonstrations and strikes from the summer of 1923 and, in Saxony and Thuringia, the SPD and KPD joined forces to win control of the state governments. The Berlin government used the Army to arrest the KPD ministers and crush the disturbances.

Threats from the Right

Many German nationalists never accepted the Weimar Republic because of the Socialist government's decision to accept the harsh terms imposed at Versailles. The conservative elites – aristocratic landowners, big industrialists and senior army officers, judges and civil servants – who had ruled Germany under the *Kaiser* largely retained their power after 1918 and they tended to be at best lukewarm in their support for the Republic. More often they were openly hostile to the democratic republic. Many favoured the restoration of the monarchy or an authoritarian alternative.

1. The Kapp *Putsch* (March 1920)

In March 1920 Wolfgang Kapp and General von Luttwitz attempted to overthrow the government. Thousands of soldiers who were about to be disbanded and returned to civilian life joined *Freikorps* units to seize control of Berlin. Kapp intended to use 12,000 of these soldiers to set up a right-wing government with himself as chancellor.

Key Term

Right-wing: term applied generally to political parties that are conservative or traditional and, in many cases, favour authoritarian government.

Key Term

Left-wing: term applied generally to political parties that favour the redistribution of wealth in society and measures such as taking major industries under public ownership.

Key Term

Spartacist: Communist political group in Germany, which took their name from the ancient Roman slave revolt leader, Spartacus.

Key Term

KPD: initials by which the German Communist Party was known.

Key Term

Putsch: German word for an attempt to seize political power by force.

The Defence Minister, Gustav Noske, ordered the *Reichswehr* (the German army) to restore order. However, the general in charge of the *Reichswehr* in Berlin, General von Seeckt, refused to order his troops to attack former soldiers. The **trade unions** organised a general strike which paralysed Berlin. After four days (12–16 March), Kapp realised he could not succeed, lacking sufficient popular support, and fled to Sweden. Over 400 *Reichswehr* officers were implicated in the *putsch* but only forty-eight were dismissed from the army.

2. The White Terror (1920–1922)

1920–1922 saw about 400 political murders, mostly committed by the extreme right, which was known as the 'White Terror', but some were carried out by the Left. The *Freikorps* were mainly responsible for this violence. In August 1921, members of the Organisation Consul, a right-wing group, composed mainly of young ex-officers, murdered Matthias Erzeberger, leader of the ZP, who had helped negotiate the armistice. In June 1922 Walther Rathenau, the foreign minister, was also assassinated by the Organisation Consul.

3. The 'Beerhall *Putsch*' (November 1923)

On 8th November Hitler took over a political meeting being addressed by von Kahr, the Bavarian State Commissioner. He announced that he was mounting a revolution to overthrow the Weimar Republic. However, Kahr escaped and the Bavarian police and army refused to support the Nazi revolution. Hitler had intended to march on Berlin once he had taken control of Bavaria. On 9th November, 2,000 SA men marched into the centre of Munich but police opened fire, sixteen Nazis were killed and Hitler was arrested later. He was tried in February 1924 and sentenced to five years in prison, but only served nine months.

What problems resulted from the Weimar Constitution?

The Weimar Constitution was drawn up between February and July 1919 by the National Constituent Assembly. It established a very advanced democratic system of government, giving all men and women over twenty the vote and strengthened the authority of the *Reichstag*, the elected house in the German Parliament. Ministers were accountable to the *Reichstag*, rather than to the head of the state, the President.

Historians broadly agree that there were certain important weaknesses in the Weimar Constitution:

1. **The voting system was proportional representation.** This system allowed very small parties to gain representation in the *Reichstag* and, because there were eight major parties in Germany and a score of smaller ones, this resulted in the *Reichstag's* seats being widely distributed among a large number of parties.

   In practice this meant that no party was ever able to gain a majority in the *Reichstag*, necessitating a series of coalition governments, consisting normally of three or more parties working together.

   These coalition governments did not last long as it proved difficult for the parties involved to keep working together. For example, 1919–1923 saw eight different government coalitions. The failure to provide stable government was a key factor in explaining why many Germans never supported the Republic and why many other Germans lost faith in the democratic system after 1929, turning to the more authoritarian alternatives promised by either the Nazis or the Communists.

2. **Article 48 of the Constitution gave the President extensive emergency powers.** He was able to suspend civil liberties in the event of an emergency, such as the outbreak of civil war. Under President Ebert (1919–1925) this did not prove a problem but President Hindenburg (1925–1934) used these emergency powers in very controversial ways:

(continued)

Key Term

Trade unions: organisations representing the interests of workers.

Key Term

Proportional representation: a voting system in which parties gain the same percentage of seats in parliament as the percentage of votes they poll in the elections.

What problems resulted from the Weimar Constitution? *(continued)*

- Between 1930 and 1932 Hindenburg used Article 48 to pass decrees implementing measures that his chancellors could not get passed through the *Reichstag*. This undermined many Germans' confidence in the democratic system.
- In February 1933 Hindenburg used Article 48 to declare a state of emergency following the *Reichstag* Fire. Hitler was then able to order the arrest of thousands of his Communist and Socialist opponents and close down their newspapers. This was an important step towards his creation of a one-party dictatorship.

1.3.2 Economic Conditions

What economic problems did the Republic face (1919–1923)?

1. There was high unemployment and low industrial output. This was largely a result of the disruption caused by a return to a peacetime economy. Many soldiers could not find work when they came back from the front.

2. Germany lost valuable mineral resources as a consequence of the Versailles Treaty. Rich coal and iron-ore deposits were handed over to Poland (e.g. Upper Silesia) and to France (e.g. Alsace-Lorraine), whilst the Saarland was put under League of Nations control for fifteen years.

3. Inflation had been a serious problem since the outbreak of the First World War. The value of the mark had declined greatly by 1919 and the governments of the period 1919–1923 were too inclined to print more paper money to finance the cost of war pensions and reparations. The Allied Reparations Committee in April 1921 had fixed reparations at the sum of 132,000 million gold marks (£6,600 million). The £6,600 million was to be paid in yearly instalments of £100 million.

Year	Marks to the £
1914	20
1919	250
1921	1000
1922	35,000
1923	16,000,000,000,000

The Hyper-Inflation Crisis (1923)

Wilhelm Cuno's government was overwhelmed by a growing crisis over reparations. Following his government's failure to hand over reparations payments in January 1923, France and Belgium decided to send 60,000 troops into the Ruhr. Cuno ordered workers in the Ruhr to go on strike.

German workers sabotaged French attempts to transport raw materials back to France and about 150 were killed in clashes with French and Belgian soldiers. The French then sealed the Ruhr off from the rest of Germany, which had disastrous effects on Germany's economy as the Ruhr produced 80% of Germany's steel and 70% of its coal. The percentage of Germans unemployed rose from 2% to 23%.

Gustav Stresemann, leader of the German People's Party (DVP), became chancellor in August 1923 and briefly led a coalition comprising the DVP, SPD, ZP and DDP.

Stresemann tackled the hyper-inflation crisis by:

- bringing in the banker Hjalmar Schacht to oversee the currency crisis. Schacht introduced a new currency, the *Rentenmark*, to replace the old mark; 1 *Rentenmark* was exchanged for 10,000,000,000,000 old marks. In 1924 the *Rentenmark* was replaced by the *Reichsmark*.

- deciding controversially to order the workers in the Ruhr to co-operate with the French and by resuming reparations payments.

What were the long-term effects of the hyper-inflation crisis?

1. Many of the middle class who lost their savings in the hyper-inflation crisis were permanently alienated from the Weimar Republic.

2. Germany suffered from a shortage of domestic investment. Many Germans lost confidence in investing in German industry and businesses following the financial crisis of 1923.

3. Germany became dangerously dependent on US loans, as a result of the Dawes Plan. The Dawes Plan (1924) helped German industry to recover in the years 1924–1928 but the Wall Street Crash of October 1929 sent the German economy into a deep economic crisis when America recalled its loans.

The Dawes Plan (August 1924)

The Dawes Plan was accepted at the London Conference; Germany was to receive an initial American loan of £40 million. Germany's reparation payments were rescheduled. In total, Germany received £3,000 million in American loans up to 1930. The French promised Germany that they would evacuate the Ruhr within a year (the last troops actually left in July 1925).

1.3.3 The 'Best Years of Weimar' (1924–1929)

Historians are divided in their assessments of the Weimar Republic in the mid to late 1920s. Some argue that the greater prosperity and stability enjoyed by Germany in these years was very superficial and would not have lasted even if Wall Street had not crashed. Others argue that the Weimar Republic was well on its way to establishing itself until the economic collapse of 1929.

What evidence was there of the Weimar Republic making progress?

(a) Economic

- In 1925 Germany entered a period of relative prosperity. The Dawes Plan of 1924 meant that Germany was receiving large loans from the USA.

- This money was used to modernise German industry; by 1928 industrial output exceeded the record 1913 figure.

- Germany's foreign exports increased by 40% in the years 1925–1929.

(b) Social

- Industrial workers' wages rose by 21% in 1927–1928 in real terms, making them the highest paid in Europe.

- Government spending on health, education and social services grew enormously; in 1913 these items made up 37% of total government expenditure, by 1932 they comprised 68%.

- Two new universities were built at Hamburg and Cologne.

- Unemployment insurance was introduced for 17 million workers in 1927.

(continued)

What evidence was there of the Weimar Republic making progress? *(continued)*

(c) Cultural

- Germany, and particularly Berlin, became a vibrant cultural centre. In architecture, the Bauhaus design movement founded by Walter Gropius was highly influential. Thomas Mann won the Nobel Prize for Literature in 1929.

(d) Political

- There were no further attempts to seize power by either the extreme left or right.
- The 1928 elections saw the political parties that were hostile to Weimar democracy losing votes:
    - The KPD's (Communists) seats fell from sixty-two to fifty-four
    - The DNVP's (Nationalists) dropped from ninety-five to seventy-three
    - The Nazis remained a tiny political force with just twelve seats.
- The moderate parties, which supported the democratic system, either made significant gains or maintained their existing levels of support, e.g. the Social Democrats (SPD) increased their seats from 100 to 153.
- From 1928 to 1930, the Grand Coalition commanded over 60% of the seats in the *Reichstag* and included the:
    - SPD (Social Democrats)
    - DDP (Democratic Party)
    - DVP (People's Party)
    - ZP (Centre)
- The election of the conservative Paul von Hindenburg as president in 1925 can be seen as a stabilising factor for the Republic as he was regarded by some of those who were hostile to the Republic as a '*Kaiser*-substitute'.

Germany's international position

Gustav Stresemann, leader of the German People's Party, wanted to see Germany make the best possible recovery from her humiliation in 1918, even if that meant first accepting the terms of the Treaty of Versailles, and then having them changed by international consent. After a brief spell as Chancellor in 1923, he became foreign minister and remained so until his death in 1929.

Stresemann's foreign policy was unpopular with nationalists but he made Germany accepted again diplomatically and won the Nobel Peace Prize in 1926 jointly with Briand, the French Foreign Minister, in recognition of their efforts to improve Franco-German relations.

 1924   Stresemann negotiated the withdrawal of the French and Belgians from the Ruhr. Stresemann helped negotiate the Dawes Plan.

 1925   At Locarno, following Stresemann's suggestion, the West European countries agreed to guarantee the frontiers of Western Europe as laid down at Versailles in 1919.

 1926   Germany was allowed to join the League of Nations.

1928 Stresemann negotiated a partial withdrawal of the Rhineland by the Allies.

1929 Stresemann negotiated the Young Plan, which reduced the total reparations bill by about two thirds. At the time of his death in October 1929, Stresemann was negotiating the final withdrawal of Allied troops from the Rhineland. This happened in 1930.

What evidence is there of continuing problems, which were to contribute to the Republic's collapse in 1933?

Economic

a. Germany was dangerously reliant on loans from the USA.

b. Unemployment never fell below 1.3 million in this period and had risen to 1.9 million by 1929 (before the Wall Street Crash).

c. Agriculture did not share in the economic boom of the mid to late 1920s. World agricultural prices were low during this period and many German farmers were undercut by more efficient competition, particularly from Canada and the USA.

Social

a. German farm workers' wages were only just over half the national average in 1929.

Political

a. The German Nationalist Party (DNVP) opposed the Young Plan because it implied that Germany still accepted her war guilt. At the end of the 1920s, the DNVP moved further to the right with the appointment of Alfred Hugenburg as their leader.

b. Similarly, the Centre Party also moved to the right under the leadership of Heinrich Bruning.

c. The 'Grand Coalition' was unstable as it contained a range of political parties from right of centre to left; in 1930 it was to collapse after the SPD argued with its Centre Party coalition partners over how to respond to the Great Depression.

1.4 Methods Used to Establish an Authoritarian State

1.4.1 Hitler's Early Years and the Creation of the Nazi Party

1889 Adolf Hitler was born in Linz in Austria, the son of a customs official.

1905 – 1913 Hitler had ambitions to become an architect, but his two applications for a place at the Academy of Fine Arts in Vienna were rejected. Consequently, he lived a rather hand-to-mouth existence in Vienna, earning a living by doing odd jobs and selling his own watercolour paintings.

Whilst in Vienna, Hitler became interested in the writings of racist authors, particularly Lanz von Liebenfels, who wrote about the supremacy of the 'Aryan' race. Hitler was a Nationalist of the racial kind. He believed that the Germans were superior to the other nationalities of the Austro-Hungarian Empire (mainly Slavs) and of the rest of the world. Vienna was full of rich Jewish businessmen, whose wealth Hitler resented. Hitler also noted the fact that many leading Socialists and Communists were Jews.

Hitler was also influenced by the writings of Charles Darwin, who had argued that the evolution of species was the result of a battle for survival in which only the fittest survived. Hitler believed that this could be applied to human societies.

Hitler moved to Munich in 1913.

1914

As a keen German nationalist, Hitler had greeted the outbreak of the First World War in 1914 with enthusiasm. Since he was living in Munich, he enlisted in the German rather than the Austro-Hungarian Army.

1918

Like most Germans, Hitler had believed that the war was going well, and the collapse in 1918 came as a great shock. Like many Germans, he assumed that Germany had been betrayed, that the Communists and the Social Democrats had 'stabbed the Fatherland in the back' and that these '**November criminals**' were to blame for Germany's defeat.

1919

In January 1919 Anton Drexler set up the German Workers' Party (DAP) in Munich; his idea was to create a party that would be both working class and nationalist. Hitler joined the tiny party in September 1919. He was put in charge of recruitment and propaganda and soon showed organisational ability and a talent for oratory.

1920

Hitler took over as party leader and the party produced a Twenty-Five Point Programme, which combined nationalist and socialist demands.

1921

Hitler set up the *Sturmabteilung* (storm-troopers) or SA, initially to protect party meetings against attacks by their enemies. They were largely recruited from former members of the *Freikorps*. Hitler saw the propaganda value of symbols and adopted the swastika as the party emblem and introduced the raised-arm salute. He also renamed the party the National Socialist German Workers Party (NSDAP).

> **⚿ Key Term**
>
> **November criminals:**
> The term used by German nationalists for the democratic politicians who signed the armistice in November 1918 when allegedly the German army could still have fought on and won the war.

1.4.2 Hitler's Role

In the early years of the Nazi movement, Hitler aimed to seize power by force. By 1923, Hitler had forged links with other right-wing groups in Bavaria. Hitler aimed to model his *putsch* on Mussolini's March on Rome, which had led to Mussolini being appointed prime minister in October 1922.

Hitler counted on gaining the support of Kahr, the Bavarian State Commissioner, and other right-wing officials in Bavaria who were hostile to the government in Berlin. However, their support was not forthcoming when Hitler attempted to take control of Munich in November 1923 and consequently the Munich *Putsch* failed, with sixteen Nazis killed and Hitler arrested. Hitler was sentenced to five years in prison but served just nine months in Landsberg prison; during his imprisonment, he dictated the first part of his autobiography, *Mein Kampf* ('My Struggle').

What did Hitler learn from the failure of the Beerhall *Putsch?*

- Crucially Hitler learned from the failure of the Munich *Putsch*; he changed his tactics – instead of seeking power through revolution, he decided to achieve power by legal means and then, once in power, establish a dictatorship. It would be necessary, as Hitler put it:

    "to hold our noses and enter the Reichstag alongside Marxist and Catholic deputies."

- Hitler also decided that the Party needed to broaden its appeal beyond that of the working class; consequently, Hitler moved increasingly away from the socialist ideas contained in the Twenty-Five Points and instead looked to win more middle-class support, with an increased emphasis on the nationalist elements of their programme.

After 1925 the *Fuhrerprinzip* (the leader principle) was strengthened. During Hitler's absence in prison, the Nazi Party had split into a number of warring factions. In 1926, Hitler successfully reasserted his authority over the Party and reorganised it.

The SA were reorganised and given greater responsibility for distributing propaganda. Hitler divided the Party organisation into *35 Gaue* (regions). In 1926 Hitler created the SS (*Schutzstaffel*), as his bodyguards, and founded the Hitler Youth.

However, Party membership was only 35,000 (1926) and in 1928 the Party gained just twelve seats in the *Reichstag* elections, less than 3% of the votes.

1.5 Short-Term Conditions That Gave Rise to an Authoritarian State in Germany

1.5.1 The Wall Street Crash of 1929

1. Impact on the German Economy

In October 1929, the USA was hit by a terrible economic crisis, which soon spread to the rest of the world. The Wall Street Crash of October 1929, which wiped millions off the value of American shares, led US investors to withdraw their money from Germany. Businesses in Germany went bankrupt, banks collapsed and people became unwilling to invest their money. The result was soaring unemployment.

Year	Unemployment
1929	2 million
1930	3.5 million
1931	4.4 million
1932 (July)	6.0 million

The Depression, unlike the crisis of 1923, was a **deflationary** crisis: prices were going down rather than up. This destroyed profit margins and caused more businesses to go bust. The value of Germany's exports fell from £630 million in 1929 to just £280 million in 1932.

2. Impact on German Politics

The Depression revived the kind of violent and unstable politics that Germany had experienced in 1918–1923. There was large-scale street violence as the paramilitary

Critical Thinking

How did the Wall Street Crash undermine the Weimar Republic and transform the fortunes of the Nazis?

Key Term

Deflationary: a situation where prices are falling, reducing profits for businesses. In the Great Depression, prices fell because of falling consumer demand.

organisations of the various political parties, particularly the Nazi SA and the Communist Red Front, fought each other. Extremist parties like the Communists grew in strength and gained more votes because people were disillusioned at the government's inability to solve the economic crisis.

Chancellor Brüning's approach to Germany's economic problems in the years 1930–1932 was traditional and cautious, he:

- Reduced government spending
- Reduced taxes
- Balanced the budget (ensured government spending was not greater than government revenue) and waited for economic conditions to improve.

To Germany's unemployed, this policy seemed callous and ineffective. Many of the jobless (and also those who were worried that they might become unemployed) turned to the extremist political parties.

In the General Election of 1930 the Nazis won 107 seats and the Communists won eighty-nine.

At a time of economic crisis, many Germans turned to Hitler as a 'messiah' figure who would save Germany in its darkest hour.

Figures for the Nazis' electoral fortunes correlate closely with unemployment levels in the period 1930–1932:

⚙ Critical Thinking

How did the Nazis become the second biggest party in Germany in 1930, and, then, in 1932 the largest?

Election date	Unemployment (in millions)	Nazi seats in the Reichstag
1930	3.5	107
July 1932	6	230

The Nazis promised to tackle unemployment through job creation schemes, which appealed more than Brüning's austerity measures, which involved cutting government spending, e.g. on welfare and unemployment benefits.

At a time of weak, unstable government, Hitler appeared to offer the prospect of strong leadership. None of the democratic parties had a leader with the charisma that Hitler possessed.

Hitler's broad appeal was demonstrated in April 1932 when he stood as a candidate against Hindenburg in the presidential election, polling 13 million votes to Hindenburg's 18 million, winning many traditional, conservative voters away from Hindenburg.

At a time when many property owners were worried about the possibility of a communist revolution, the Nazis, with their 700,000 strong SA (*Stürm Abteilung*/Stormtroopers), seemed to promise greater security than the government could provide.

The SA disrupted the activities of opposition parties, breaking up their rallies, and they engaged in violent battles with armed supporters of other parties, particularly the Communists. In doing so, they helped create a climate of violence and an impression that the democratic system of government could not maintain public order.

They appealed to small farmers/peasants who were struggling with debts, falling food prices and competition from bigger, more commercial farmers. The Nazis promised to protect them and provide subsidies.

The Nazis gained the votes of many lower middle-class Germans such as teachers, shop-keepers, and civil servants who were not necessarily unemployed but feared they might end up so.

Many historians have suggested the Nazis picked up little working-class support and, while it is true that most workers in the big cities continued to vote for the SPD or KPD, the Nazis did win significant working-class converts as shown by their predominance within the SA.

Marxist historians have portrayed Hitler as the puppet of big business, arguing that it was their financial support that made possible Nazi electoral success. It is certainly true that the Nazis did receive financial backing from some leading industrialists from 1930 onwards but this was limited before Hitler became Chancellor as many industrialists were worried by the socialist slogans of the more left-wing members of the NSDAP.

The Nazis presented an image of dynamism and youth. Their campaigning tactics were more modern that those of other parties, e.g. Hitler flew to many cities in the 1932 elections. Mass rallies created for many Germans a sense of belonging.

Nazi **propaganda**, skilfully orchestrated by Goebbels, targeted different groups with different messages offering:

- Subsidies to peasants
- Law and order and a return to traditional values to the middle classes
- Jobs for unemployed workers
- A defence against communist revolution and the revival of Germany as a great power to conservative nationalists.

 **Key Term**

Propaganda: the spreading of ideas or information by a party or person aiming to promote its own cause.

At the same time, the Nazis promised to unite the country. They provided scapegoats for Germany's problems:

- The Jews (although some historians suggest that the Nazis played down their anti-Semitic message in the early 1930s)
- The democratic system
- The Communists
- The victor powers in the First World War.

> **None of this was new, so why did these messages prove more effective in the 1930s than in the 1920s?**
>
> - Disillusionment with the Weimar Republic and democratic parties was far greater, as was the scale of Germany's economic problems.
> - Hitler had created a more respectable image for the Nazis after his release from prison and was therefore able to win more middle-class support.

1.5.2 The Breakdown of Democratic Government (1930–1932)

Normal democratic government broke down because no government between 1930 and 1932 could command a majority in the *Reichstag*. Under Article 48 of the Weimar Constitution, the president could declare a state of emergency and govern by decree, without consulting parliament.

President Paul von Hindenburg had no sympathy with the Weimar Republic; he was a traditional Nationalist and sympathised with Hugenburg's DNVP. He regarded the

Nazis as radical thugs, but he hated the Social Democrats and Communists even more and was alarmed at the growing strength of the Communists.

1930 Hindenburg dismissed Chancellor Müller's government and appointed Heinrich von Brüning of the Centre Party. Brüning had very limited support in the *Reichstag* but was able to remain in power in the period 1930–1932 because Hindenburg used his emergency powers to pass the laws that Brüning requested.

1932 By 1932, Hindenburg was tired of having to support Brüning's weak government and so replaced Brüning with the conservative Franz von Papen. Von Papen, however, commanded even less support in the *Reichstag*, so Hindenburg agreed to call a General Election in July. The result was a triumph for the Nazis who won 230 seats.

Why did Hindenburg not appoint Hitler as chancellor in the summer of 1932?

- After the July 1932 elections, the Nazis were the biggest single party in the *Reichstag* and no coalition government could be formed without them. President Hindenburg was anxious to get back to a situation in which the government had a parliamentary majority. Such a government would be better able to resist the Communist threat and would also be able to take firm action on the issues of the Versailles Treaty and the economic crisis.

- Hindenburg tried to persuade Hitler to join a coalition but Hitler would only do so if he could be chancellor. Hindenburg, who disliked Hitler and feared the SA, was not yet ready to agree to this.

Instead Hindenburg called a second election in November 1932. The Nazis' share of seats dropped to 196, but they remained the largest party. Impatient because von Papen was unable to form an effective coalition, Hindenburg sacked him in November 1932 and replaced him with General Kurt von Schleicher.

Why did the Nazi Party face a crisis in the autumn of 1932?

- By the end of 1932, Nazi morale was low following their loss of seats in the November election.

- Party funds were exhausted as a result of fighting two parliamentary elections and a presidential election in a single year.

- Some of Hitler's supporters, especially the SA leadership, were impatient with Hitler's legal approach to gaining power and wanted to stage an armed rising.

- Furthermore, General von Schleicher tried to win the support of the more left-wing Nazis and thereby split the Party.

- However, Schleicher's overtures to Strasser and other more 'left-wing' Nazis failed and Hitler was able to reassert his leadership over the Party. A Nazi businessman, von Schröder, persuaded a number of his business contacts to make significant contributions to Nazi funds. President Hindenburg quickly fell out with Chancellor von Schleicher, who was unable to command a majority in parliament. Von Papen plotted with Hindenburg against Schleicher.

Why did Hindenburg appoint Hitler as chancellor on 30ᵗʰ January 1933?

- By January 1933 Hindenburg had decided that the only way to achieve a majority coalition was by offering Hitler the chancellorship. In fact, Hindenburg was happier to offer Hitler the post of Chancellor now that the Nazis' position was somewhat weaker than it had been before November 1932.

- Hindenburg's offer was based on only three of the eleven cabinet members being Nazis; Von Papen would be vice-chancellor and several members of the conservative DNVP would be included in the cabinet. Hindenburg believed that he and his conservative political allies would be able to control Hitler.

1.6 Hitler's Establishment of an Authoritarian State

1.6.1 From Chancellor to Dictator (1933–1934)

Within six months of being appointed chancellor, Hitler had outmanoeuvred his conservative cabinet colleagues and set up a single party-state.

Jan 1933

Hitler appointed Chancellor.
Three Nazi ministers in the Cabinet of eleven ministers.

Feb 1933

Hermann Goering, a leading Nazi, was given control of the Prussian police, which he used to bring in 50,000 extra police (mainly SA). Goering used the purged police force to arrest opponents of the Nazis.

The *Reichstag* Fire; the *Reichstag* (parliament building) burnt down. This was blamed on the Communists. President Hindenburg declared a state of emergency and Communist and trade union leaders were arrested. The Decree for the Protection of People and State suspended civil liberties and led to the virtual destruction of the Communist Party. This made it much easier for Hitler to get the Enabling Act passed in March, by which he acquired the power to bypass the *Reichstag*.

March 1933

Reichstag elections—Nazis won 44% of seats, Nationalists won 8%.
The Enabling Act was passed—Communist deputies were in prison; the Centre voted in favour of the change to the constitution after Hitler promised to leave the Catholic Church alone. Hitler was now able to by-pass the *Reichstag* in making laws.
A law was issued to co-ordinate the state parliaments; all now had a Nazi majority. In 1934 Hitler abolished all state parliaments.

April 1933

Hitler replaced all eighteen state governors with Nazis.

May 1933

Trade unions were banned-they were replaced by the German Labour Front (a Nazi organisation).

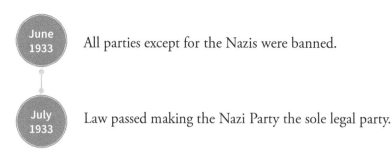

All parties except for the Nazis were banned.

Law passed making the Nazi Party the sole legal party.

1.6.2 Hitler's Consolidation of Power

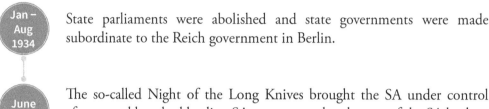

Jan – Aug 1934
State parliaments were abolished and state governments were made subordinate to the Reich government in Berlin.

June 1934
The so-called Night of the Long Knives brought the SA under control after several hundred leading SA were arrested and many of the SA leaders, including Ernst Rohm, were executed.

Hitler claimed the SA leaders had been plotting a putsch. There is no evidence of this; once in power, Hitler found the SA leaders a liability as they demanded a 'second revolution' which would see big businesses nationalised and the army swallowed up in a people's army led by the SA. Hitler needed to secure his links with the Army and big business in order to rearm and expand Germany's borders.

Aug 1934
Following President Hindenburg's death, Hitler required the Army to take an oath of allegiance to him. Hitler also merged the offices of president and chancellor, making himself Führer ('Leader').

Were the Party and State fully integrated?

- Many Nazis wanted the Party to take over state institutions at every level, but this never happened.
- Weimar institutions remained except for the *Reichsrat* (upper house of Parliament) and the *Landtage* (state parliaments), which were abolished.
- The civil service was purged in 1933—under the Law for the Restoration of a Professional Civil Service—but not until 1939 was party membership made compulsory for civil servants.
- Until 1937 a majority of government ministers were non-Nazis e.g. von Neurath (Foreign Minister), von Blomberg (War Minister)—but in 1937/1938 most non-Nazis were removed (e.g. Neurath was replaced by Ribbentrop) as Hitler began to accelerate his plans for territorial expansion. By 1936, Himmler controlled all police forces in Germany.
- The Army (*Wehrmacht*) escaped co-ordination by the Nazis; the SA leaders had wanted to create a mass, revolutionary 'people's army' resulting from the absorption of the *Wehrmacht* by the SA. Hitler rejected this and the generals were relieved and grateful when Hitler purged the SA in June 1934. In early 1938, Hitler removed eighteen senior generals, including Blomberg and Fritsch (commander-in-chief) and assumed personal command of the armed forces.

TOPICS:
Long-term conditions
Short-term conditions
Methods

Gleichschaltung (co-ordination)

The Nazis aimed to 'co-ordinate' every aspect of the German population's lives so that they conformed to the Nazis' ideals. Force and persuasion were used by the Nazis in their drive to 'Nazify' Germany politically, socially and culturally.

2.1 Use of Terror

The Third Reich was certainly a police state with the Gestapo, SD, SS, a purged police and legal system, eighteen concentration camps and a vicious punishment code.

2.1.1 The Legal System

The Nazis replaced the old Weimar legal system, which emphasised people's rights and freedoms, with a new system which placed the race and the community above the individual. Under this new system of law the highest duty of a citizen was obedience to the *Führer*, and to show disrespect for Hitler was a crime. Judges had to swear an oath of allegiance to Hitler and, as part of Hitler's co-ordination of every aspect of German life, no one could practise as a lawyer unless they belonged to the League of National Socialist German Lawyers (BNSDJ).

The Decree for the Protection of People and State (February 1933) allowed indefinite detention without trial.

In 1934, the People's Court was set up to deal with treasonable offences. The court's proceedings, presided over by Roland Freisler, were secret and there was no right of appeal (except to Hitler).

2.1.2 Concentration Camps

Dachau, the first concentration camp, opened in March 1933. There were never fewer than 10,000 prisoners in the camps and, in total, probably about 225,000 Germans were imprisoned for political crimes in the years 1933–1939. Until the Night of the Long Knives (June 1934), the camps were run by the SA; but, from 1934 onwards, the

🔑 Key Term

Gleichschaltung: process by which the Nazis aimed to bring every aspect of the lives of German citizens into line with Nazi ideas, either closing down non-Nazi organisations or imposing Nazi control over them.

SS were placed in charge of them. Discipline in the camps was brutal, the diet poor and living conditions inadequate. Prisoners were made to do hard labour, and were subjected to sadistic beatings and torture.

Figure 2.1: *Prisoners barracks at Dachau Concentration Camp.*

2.1.3 Policing and Security Forces

Alongside the ordinary police forces whose jobs were to detect crime and keep order, a new system of political policing developed. Both systems came under the control of Heinrich Himmler, the *Reichsführer* of the SS.

Hermann Goering set up the Gestapo in Prussia in 1933; Heinrich Himmler took control of the Gestapo after 1933. From 1936 onwards, Himmler was in control of all police and security forces. The Gestapo was heavily dependent on denunciations by ordinary Germans, e.g. in Wurzberg 54% of all race-related charges were initiated by private citizens.

The Gestapo and the Security Service (SD) rooted out and dealt with political offenders and opponents of the regime. The SD was set up in 1931 by Himmler; increasingly they were given the task of gathering intelligence and monitoring public opinion.

The SS

The SS was created in 1925, coming under Himmler's control in 1929, and became immensely powerful after the Night of the Long Knives. It had 200,000 members by 1935. The Death's Head units of the SS ran the concentration camps from 1934, taking over from the SA.

Himmler also built up the Waffen SS, regiments of SS soldiers who had a higher standard of training than members of the ordinary German Army and were better equipped with tanks and motorised vehicles.

During the Second World War, the SS took control of many factories, manufacturing everything from carved furniture to ammunition and even bottling fizzy drinks. The SS became a kind of state within the state and played a major part in ruling territories conquered by the Nazis and in carrying out what Himmler called the 'Final Solution of the Jewish Question'. *Einsatzgruppen* units of the SS rounded up and killed thousands of Jews, gypsies and Slavs in Poland and Russia from the autumn of 1939 onwards.

2.2 Propaganda and Control of the Media

2.2.1 Charismatic leadership: The *Führer* Cult

A cult of the *Führer* was established; for example, the book *The Hitler No One Knows* sold 420,000 copies between 1932–1940. Hitler's birthday was celebrated with mass rallies and parades. The historian Ian Kershaw argues that Hitler was increasingly a victim of the '*Führer* myth' and began to confuse fantasy and reality, especially in foreign policy.

2.2.2 Propaganda, Control of the Media and Culture

The media and arts were controlled. In March 1933, the Ministry for Popular Enlightenment and Propaganda was set up by Josef Goebbels.

Goebbels regarded radio as the most important medium; the Reich Radio Company brought all broadcasting under Nazi control. A cheap radio, the *Volksepfanger,* was mass-produced; in 1932 fewer than 25% households had a radio, by 1939 more than 70% did.

In 1933 there were 4,700 daily papers in Germany, by 1944 only 1,000. Eher Verlag (the Nazi publishing house) controlled 66% of the Press by 1939. The sole news agency permitted was run by the Nazis.

All films had to pass censors and about half of Germany's best-known film stars emigrated.

Nazi ritual assumed religious dimensions. New rituals were created to celebrate the Nazi state: the Nuremberg rallies, celebrations of the Munich *Putsch* and Hitler's birthday.

The Nazis stood for the traditional in art, music, literature and drama and they, in common with many ordinary Germans, were puzzled by and hostile to the highly experimental culture of which Berlin was a centre in the 1920s. This disgust for 'modern' art was made clear by Adolf Ziegler, the President of the Reich Chamber of Art, in a speech he made in 1937 at the opening of the 'House of German Art' in Munich:

> "It is clear that the eye of some men portrays things otherwise than they are, that there really are men who on principle feel meadows to be blue, the heaven green, clouds sulphur-yellow, or, as perhaps they prefer to say, 'experience' them thus. If they do not believe in the reality of such impressions but seek on other grounds to burden the nation with this humbug, then it is a matter for a criminal court. The artist does not create for the artist, he creates for the people."

Ziegler and other Nazis objected to the abstract and expressionist painting that had been fashionable in Germany in the 1920s. They wanted a return to a style that was more realistic, and they wanted artists to concentrate on certain themes.

Adolf Ziegler organised an exhibition of the kind of paintings of which the Nazis disapproved, calling it the Exhibition of Degenerate Art. He and other Nazis blamed the Jews and the Communists for the spread of this kind of art, and regarded it as part of a conspiracy to undermine German 'culture'.

The Nazis also wanted a literature and drama which would reflect their ideas, and, in May 1933, Goebbels organised 'The burning of the books' in Berlin. Libraries were ransacked for books by authors of whom the Nazis disapproved, and Goebbels himself addressed the students who hurled the books into a public bonfire on the Unter den Linden, the main street in Berlin.

"Fellow students! German men and women! The age of extreme Jewish intellectualism has now ended, and the success of the German revolution has given the right of way to the German spirit. You are doing the right things in committing the evil spirit of the past to the flames at this late hour of the night. It is a strong, symbolic act."

As the students threw books onto the bonfire they chanted slogans, such as:

"Against class struggle and materialism

For the national community and an idealistic outlook."

[For the books of Karl Marx.]

"Against the debasing exaggeration of man's animal nature

For the nobility of the human soul."

[For the books of Sigmund Freud.]

Against literary betrayal of the soldiers of the World War

For the education of the nation in the spirit of military preparedness."

[For the books of Erich Maria Remarque.]

Remarque was the author of the powerful novel *All Quiet on the Western Front*, an indictment of the First World War and of aggressive nationalism.

In architecture, the Nazis favoured a massive, classical style based on that of ancient Greece and Rome, and they rejected the modern style. Hitler himself was fascinated by architecture and spent happy hours with his personal architect, Albert Speer, planning the rebuilding of Berlin.

In music Hitler's preference was for 19th century classical music, particularly the operas of Richard Wagner and the operettas of Franz Lehar. He disliked the modern experimental music of composers such as Stravinsky and Arnold Schoenberg and banned the works of traditional Jewish composers such as Mendelssohn.

Artists, writers and composers had to join Nazi organisations in order to pursue their art, and refusal to join these Nazi organisations meant that it was impossible to get their work displayed, published or performed. All publications were censored by the government, and the censors looked not so much at the contents of the book as at the political views, character and race of its author. The general effect of all this censorship and control was to produce an art, literature and music that were boring and unadventurous—endless paintings or plays about virtuous peasant families and their day to day problems.

2.3 Raising Living Standards

2.3.1 The German Labour Front

Hitler abolished the trade unions in May 1933 and made it compulsory for all workers to join the German Labour Front (DAF), a Nazi organisation headed by Dr Robert Ley. Special committees called the Trustees of Labour were established to settle disputes between workers and employers about wages and working conditions. In general, the Trustees tended to side with the employers.

Nevertheless, most workers enjoyed a higher standard of living under the Nazis in the years 1933–1939. Unemployment fell from nearly six million in 1932 to only a few hundred thousand by 1939, and those in work found that their wages were higher than they had been in the last years of the Weimar Republic although not as much as in 1928 (the peak year of the Weimar Republic's economic prosperity).

The German Labour Front also took over responsibility for the workers' leisure and recreation. Non-Nazi recreational clubs were often closed down, even chess clubs. Ley set up two new organisations called 'Beauty of Labour' and 'Strength through Joy' (KDF). 'Beauty of Labour' campaigned to persuade employers to provide better working conditions, factory canteens and proper lighting and ventilation. Some of the activities organised by Strength through Joy and the number of participants are shown below, illustrating the scale of working-class Germans' involvement.

KDF activity	Number of participants
Concerts	2.5 million
Theatre	7.4 million
Gymnastic clubs	2.5 million
Holiday outings	1.4 million
Hikes	1.9 million

KDF also launched a scheme to design and mass produce a cheap car that ordinary workers could afford to buy. It was originally called the KDF-wagen, but later became known as the People's Car (Volkswagen). The prototype of the model, later known as the 'Beetle', was produced just before the Second World War broke out, but production was then halted until after the war.

2.4 Dealing with Opposition

Opposition to the Nazis has received more attention from historians over the past twenty-five years; as historians have come to realise that the Nazi system was less efficient than had been traditionally believed, they have become increasingly aware of opposition to the Nazis. Grumbling and minor dissent, especially over lack of wage rises and increases in working hours, were quite widespread. Reports compiled by SOPADE (the SPD in exile) indicate that most grumbling was the result of economic conditions.

2.4.1 Continuing Opposition from the Left

- The working class posed a real challenge to the Nazis in that they made up 45% of the population and had tended to support the SPD and KPD before 1933.

- The SPD had 1 million members in 1933 and 4 million associate members within the trade unions. The Nazis arrested many socialists in 1933 but some of the SPD leaders operated from exile (SOPADE), first from Prague and, from 1938, from Paris. SOPADE's activities were mainly intelligence gathering and its policy after 1933 was to wait for the collapse of the Nazi regime.

- The KPD were more active in their opposition; by 1939 KPD organisations existed in eighty-nine Berlin factories. There was rising working class dissatisfaction in the period 1937–1939 because of the failure to win substantial pay rises. The KPD tried to undermine the Nazi regime by distributing leaflets.

- Both the SPD and KPD smuggled pamphlets into Germany; 1.6 million were seized at the border in 1935 and in 1934–1936 200,000 people in Germany were able to read each edition of 'Socialist Action' (SPD). However, their leadership had been seriously hit by the mass arrests following the *Reichstag* Fire. Ten thousand communists had been arrested and thereafter the KPD operated in very small cells and concerted action was, therefore, very difficult. Left-wing opposition to the Nazis continued to be hampered by the ongoing conflict between the SPD and KPD.

2.4.2 Opposition from the Churches

Opposition to the Nazis from the churches was limited but 693 Catholic priests were arrested for opposition in the years 1939–1943, while a much smaller number of Protestant pastors (around fifty) were imprisoned and the churches clashed with the Nazi regime on several occasions:

- Pastor Niemoller led the opposition to the attempt by the Nazis to centralise all the Protestant churches into a single *Reich* Church in 1933.

- There were widespread Catholic protests against the order to replace crucifixes by portraits of Hitler in Catholic schools, for example in the Rhineland in 1937 and in Bavaria in 1941, and, in both instances, the Nazi authorities backed down and cancelled the order for their removal.

- Cardinal von Galen preached a sermon in 1941 against the secret euthanasia programme in which tens of thousands of disabled adults and children were killed. Copies of the sermon were widely distributed.

2.4.3 Opposition from within the Army

Many officers welcomed Nazi rearmament policies but some senior officers had serious misgivings about Hitler's foreign policy. Before the outbreak of war the only significant opposition to emerge within the Army was that centring on Ludwig Beck, Chief of Staff, who, in 1938, conspired to bring down Hitler during the Sudeten crisis. Beck's plotting against Hitler proved ineffective and military opposition disappeared until defeat in the Second World War seemed inevitable.

2.4.4 Growing Opposition after 1939

During the Second World War, a variety of resistance groups emerged:

- The White Rose group at Munich University, led by Sophie and Hans Scholl, who were executed in 1943 for distributing anti-Nazi leaflets.

- Conservatives such as Carl Goerdeler, the Mayor of Leipzig, co-operated with the plots against Hitler laid by army officers. Many of these resistance workers were members of the secret Kreisau Circle which met at the house of Count von Moltke. The Kreisau Circle aimed to draw up plans for the period after Hitler's downfall rather than trying to bring it about. Moltke was arrested in 1944 and other members of the group then linked up with Stauffenberg.

- The Stauffenberg Bomb Plot of July 1944, which came close to killing Hitler, had significant backing from senior officers who sought to bring about a negotiated peace with the Allies. Colonel Claus von Stauffenberg placed a bomb in a briefcase under the table where Hitler was attending a meeting. Hitler was injured in the explosion but survived. 5,000 people were executed after the Bomb Plot. By 1945, 500,000 Germans were in concentration camps.

Why was opposition to the Nazi regime so limited?

- There was much positive support for the regime, and especially for Hitler himself. This was partly the result of Goebbels' propaganda machine but mainly because the regime delivered results particularly in terms of tackling unemployment and in foreign policy.
- Hitler was seen by many Germans as a moderate who would tame radical Nazis like Ernst Röhm, and, in his early years in power, Hitler constantly stressed in his speeches that he sought peace.
- Organised centres of opposition were destroyed in 1933—rival political parties, trade unions etc.
- Opposition was illegal and because of the fear inspired by the SS and Gestapo. Terror was effective because, although it affected only a minority, it made the majority unwilling to speak out about issues that they did not feel immediately affected them.

The theologian Dietrich Bonhoeffer bravely spoke out about the failure of others to speak up against Nazi injustice in a sermon he preached in 1937:

"First they came for the Jews and I did not speak out because I was not a Jew.

Then they came for the Communists and I did not speak out because I was not a Communist.

Next they came for the trade unionists and I did not speak out because I was not a trade unionist.

Then they came for me and there was no one left to speak out for me."

2.5 The Impact of Foreign Policy on Hitler's Maintenance of Power

Hitler's Foreign Policies	Impact on Maintenance of Power
One of the key aspects of Hitler's appeal to German voters in the early 1930s was his promise to put right the wrongs committed against Germany by the Treaty of Versailles and to restore Germany to the great power status it had enjoyed up to 1918. Once in power, Hitler pursued an increasingly dynamic foreign power which helped cement the loyalty of many Germans to his regime. Hitler's breaches of the Versailles Treaty, such as the remilitarisation of the Rhineland in 1936, and his rapid rearmament contributed to a growing sense of national self-confidence.	POSITIVE
While it is clear that most Germans supported Hitler's expansionist foreign policy, particularly the union with Austria in 1938, it seems that many were anxious about the prospect of war. This was evident at the time of the war scare of September 1938 when it seemed likely that war might break out between Germany and Czechoslovakia and, potentially France and Britain, over the Sudetenland and led to a number of senior German officers conspiring against Hitler. Yet, that war scare blew over and most Germans seem to have welcomed Hitler's absorption of the Sudetenland and dismemberment of Czechoslovakia in 1938–1939.	UNCLEAR
Hitler's invasion of Poland in September 1939, leading to war with France and Great Britain, seems at first to have undermined many Germans' confidence in Hitler's leadership. However, the rapid defeat of Poland and Hitler's brilliant *Blitzkrieg* victories against Norway, Denmark, Holland, Belgium and France in 1940 stimulated German patriotic feeling and boosted support for Hitler's regime.	POSITIVE
This situation only began to change from late 1941 when Hitler failed to defeat the USSR in a short campaign and instead Germany became mired in an atrocious war of attrition on the Eastern Front. As German military losses mounted and the USA entered the war in December 1941, resistance within Germany to the Nazi regime increased, though never to the point of being able to overthrow it.	NEGATIVE
With Hitler refusing to cut his losses and withdraw from the USSR and Germany subjected to massive American and British bombing, resistance grew more extensive, with the most serious internal threat to Hitler coming from within his own officer corps, culminating in the Stauffenberg Plot of 1944. Ultimately, Hitler's impending defeat in the Second World War led to the collapse of the Nazi regime following his suicide in April 1945.	NEGATIVE

2.5.1 Hitler's Foreign Policy Aims

What are the main sources of evidence for Hitler's foreign policy aims?

- The Twenty-Five Points (1920)
- *Mein Kampf* (1924/1925)
- Hitler's *Second Book* (1928) – unpublished
- The Four Year Plan Memorandum (1936)
- The Hossbach Memorandum (1937).

> **Key Historical Perspectives:** What were Hitler's foreign policy goals?
>
> The historian AJP Taylor argued that when Hitler came to power he had no precise goals, just a desire for expansion and that his foreign policy thereafter was shaped purely by opportunism.
>
> Historians such as Hugh Trevor-Roper reject this view, arguing that from 1924–1925 onwards, when Hitler wrote *Mein Kampf*, clear objectives are evident, which Hitler then put into effect in the 1930s.
>
> It seems certain that Hitler did not have a detailed blueprint or timetable for expansion but what stands out is that he had decisively rejected more traditional German nationalists' goal of a return to the borders of 1914. Instead, driven by his racialist theories, Hitler sought **lebensraum** (living space) in the east as his main aim. Fritz Fischer has argued for continuity between German foreign policy pre-1914 and pre-1939, but other historians point to the unique racial element in Nazi foreign policy.

Foreign policy was of primary importance to Hitler. His main priority from 1934, once he had established his dictatorship, was to rearm Germany.

- Revising the Versailles Treaty was for Hitler not the ultimate goal but a means towards the larger aim of winning **lebensraum**; breaking the restrictions that Versailles had imposed on Germany's armed forces was a prerequisite for expansion.

- Hitler's racist ideas meant that he was committed to the creation of a 'Greater' Germany, incorporating all German-speakers. However, he wanted to go much further than that; he sought *lebensraum* for the German **Aryan 'master race'** and also to seize areas which had the resources that Germany needed: *Grosswirtschaftsraum*: 'Greater Economic space'.

  Hitler envisaged a Germany which would include the whole of Eastern Europe and the western part of the USSR. The native peoples of the area, mainly Slavs and regarded by the Nazis as '*untermenschen*' (sub-human), would work for the Germans as slaves.

2.5.2 Early Foreign Policy Successes

Initially Hitler had to proceed cautiously because in 1933 Germany's armed forces were considerably weaker than those of its neighbours such as France and Poland. However, from 1936 onwards, the pace of Hitler's foreign policy accelerated sharply, causing his cautious generals great anxiety.

In 1933 Hitler withdrew Germany from the League of Nations and from the League's Disarmament Conference, using France's refusal to allow German rearmament as an excuse. Hitler sought to win British support by claiming that he was prepared to accept a limit of 200,000 for the German Army.

Hitler signed a friendship treaty with Poland in 1934, thus reassuring many Germans who hoped that Hitler would, along with putting right the wrongs of Versailles, maintain peace in Europe.

The Dollfuss *Putsch* (July 1934)

In July 1934, the Austrian Nazis tried to seize power in Vienna in order to achieve the *Anschluss* (union with Germany), and murdered the Austrian chancellor, Engelbert Dollfuss. The *putsch* failed and Kurt Schuschnigg, an opponent of the Nazis, became chancellor. The incident alarmed Mussolini, who had had close relations with Dollfuss, so much that he mobilised Italian troops at the Brenner Pass, on the Austro-Italian border. Most contemporaries believed that Hitler was behind the attempted Austrian Nazi *putsch* but historians are divided over this question.

🔑 Key Term

Lebensraum **(living-space):** Hitler argued that Germany lacked the space and resources to sustain its current population and therefore needed to achieve more 'living space' in Eastern Europe at the expense of the 'inferior' Slavic peoples of that region.

🔑 Key Term

Aryan 'master race': the Nazis believed that most Germans belonged to a wider racial group, the so-called 'Aryan race', that predominated in northern Europe. They believed in a hierarchy of races, with the Aryan race at the top.

Revisions of the Versailles Treaty (1935)

Reunion with the Saar

In January, the inhabitants of the Saar, run by the League of Nations since 1920, voted by a vast majority in favour of reunion with Germany. This boosted Hitler's popularity in Germany and strengthened Germany's economy because the Saar was a major coal mining region.

The reintroduction of conscription and Hitler's announcement of rearmament

In March, Hitler announced that he was reintroducing military **conscription** and that he intended to create an army of 550,000 men. He also revealed that Germany already had begun to build, in breach of Versailles, an air force. Again, these moves appear to have boosted domestic support for Hitler because many Germans believed the recreation of a strong army was essential for both Germany's security and for reviving its status as a great power.

> **⌕ Key Term**
>
> **Conscription:** compulsory military service.

A show of opposition to Nazi expansion: the Stresa Front (April 1935)

Immediately after Hitler's reintroduction of conscription, he was faced with what was potentially a serious obstacle to his expansionist plans; the leaders of Britain, France and Italy met at Stresa and agreed that they would take collective action in the event of further German breaches of Versailles.

However, the Stresa Front quickly broke down because:

- Britain angered France and Italy by signing the Anglo-German Naval Agreement in June 1935, allowing Germany to have a navy with a tonnage of 35% that of Britain.
- In October 1935 Mussolini launched an attack on Abyssinia, which angered Britain and France and completed the collapse of the Stresa Front, after Britain and France had unsuccessfully and, rather half-heartedly, tried to get Mussolini to withdraw.

> **⌕ Key Term**
>
> **Appeasement:** the policy of trying to maintain peace by making concessions to a potentially aggressive state.

Why did Britain and France choose to appease Hitler between 1936 and 1938?

- The British Government had decided that some of the Versailles Treaty's restrictions on Germany were unreasonably harsh, and that making concessions to Hitler would make Hitler behave more reasonably and thus maintain peace in Europe. This assumption was the basis of the British policy of **'appeasement'** for the next four years.
- French leaders were opposed to German breaches of the Versailles Treaty but believed France was too weak to prevent them unless Britain took joint action alongside her.
- British politicians, on the other hand, were more favourably disposed towards German revisions of the treaty as long as this was done through negotiation.
- France was politically very divided in the 1930s; many on the Right in France were more concerned about the French Communist Party and the threat of Soviet expansion than about Hitler.
- Britain and France were preoccupied with resolving the economic problems caused by the Wall Street Crash.

Britain and France's reluctance to take action against Nazi Germany allowed Hitler to make serious breaches in the Treaty of Versailles in the period up to 1939 and these foreign policy successes bolstered support for Hitler.

Remilitarising the Rhineland (March 1936)

Hitler generally proved adept at reading how his opponents were likely to respond. Encouraged by the collapse of the Stresa Front, and by the international community's preoccupation with the Abyssinian crisis, he felt confident enough to remilitarise the Rhineland, a breach of both the Versailles Treaty and the Locarno Pact (1925) under which Germany had agreed that the Rhineland should be a **demilitarised zone.** Although the League of Nations condemned this action, France and Britain did nothing about it.

Hitler's generals were astonished; they had advised against the move, believing it would provoke a war with the much larger French Army. Again, this breach of Versailles was welcomed by most Germans as a restoration of Germany's full sovereignty.

Growing ties with Fascist Italy

During 1936 and 1937 Hitler worked to strengthen relations with Italy:

- Hitler and Mussolini both sent troops and planes to fight alongside the forces of the rebel Nationalist General, Francisco Franco in the Spanish Civil War (1936–1939).

- During the Abyssinian crisis (1935–1936), Germany continued to trade with Italy in spite of League imposed sanctions on Italy.

- In October 1936 Hitler and Mussolini signed the Rome-Berlin Axis, a friendship treaty.

The Hossbach Memorandum (November 1937)

In November 1937, Hitler held a meeting with key military and diplomatic personnel, at which he outlined his plans for '*lebensraum*' ('living space'), which he said that Germany needed to achieve by 1943–1945. Hitler spoke about the need to achieve *Anschluss* (union) with Austria and to destroy Czechoslovakia. Colonel Hossbach made a record of the meeting which is known as the 'Hossbach Memorandum'.

Some of Hitler's more cautious generals and diplomatic officials, who were non-Nazis, expressed their concerns at his expansionist plans. Over the next few months, Hitler removed these doubters, including Neurath, the Foreign Minister, and Blomberg, the War Minister. In addition, eighteen generals were obliged to retire. Hitler had now very largely cut his links with the military and diplomatic personnel he had inherited from the Weimar Republic.

Achieving the *Anschluss* (March 1938)

In February 1938 Hitler summoned Austria's chancellor, Kurt Schuschnigg, to a meeting at Berchtesgaden and bullied him into making concessions including the appointment of a leading Austrian Nazi, Artur Seyss-Inquart, as interior minister.

Once he returned to Vienna, Schuschnigg tried to regain the initiative by announcing a **plebiscite** (referendum) would be held in which the Austrian people would vote on whether they wanted Austria to remain *"a free and German, independent, Christian and united"* country. Hitler, fearing that an unsupervised plebiscite might go against him, used the threat of force to compel President Miklas to sack Schuschnigg in favour of Seyss-Inquart, who immediately invited German troops into Austria. Following a bloodless invasion on 12 March, the *Anschluss* was proclaimed. In a Nazi-supervised plebiscite, 99% of those who voted expressed their approval of the *Anschluss*.

🔑 Key Term

Demilitarised zone: the Versailles Treaty laid down that Germany could neither station troops nor build fortifications in the Rhineland, which bordered France.

🔑 Key Term

Plebiscite: a referendum or vote taken by a population over one issue or question.

Neither Britain nor France had the will to resist Hitler, partly because there were many in both countries who regarded Hitler's desire for a greater Germany as reasonable—as did most Germans.

The Sudeten Crisis (September 1938)

It seems clear that Hitler sought to pick a quarrel with the Czech government over the Sudetenland in order to provide an excuse for invading Czechoslovakia and destroying it. Hitler saw the Czechs as an inferior race and had resented them since his time growing up within the old Austro-Hungarian Empire. Czechoslovakia had been created by the hated 1919–1920 peace settlement and included over 3 million Sudeten Germans who had, in Hitler's eyes, been denied the **right of self-determination.**

In seeking to gain control of Czechoslovakia, Hitler encouraged the Sudeten German Party led by Henlein to keep on raising its demands in order to prevent an agreement between the Czech government and the Sudeten Germans.

Britain's Prime Minister Neville Chamberlain still believed that Hitler wanted nothing more than a Greater German *Reich* and that peace could be maintained by appeasing him.

Sept 15 — Chamberlain visited Hitler at Berchtesgaden and, during the next week, he and French Prime Minister Daladier devised a plan under which Czechoslovakia would be made to hand over any territory where more than 50% of the inhabitants were German to Germany.

Sept 22 — Chamberlain met Hitler again at Bad Godesberg. Hitler then raised his demands by asking for immediate occupation of the Sudetenland. War seemed imminent, and the Czechs and their French allies began to mobilise. The Poles and the Hungarians, encouraged by Hitler, also began to demand that parts of Czechoslovakia should be handed over to them.

Sept 29 — Chamberlain, in a last bid to preserve the peace, appealed to Mussolini who persuaded Hitler to attend a conference, along with Daladier of France, at Munich. The Czechs were not consulted and their other ally, the USSR, was not invited. It was agreed that Hitler should occupy the Sudetenland in stages rather than all at once. Since France, the USSR, and Britain were not prepared to support them and they could not win a single-handed war against Germany, the Czechs were forced to agree to this. In return Hitler signed a non-committal document expressing a desire for a lasting Anglo-German peace.

The hollowness of appeasement revealed: Hitler seized the rest of Czechoslovakia and Memel (March 1939)

Chamberlain and Daladier soon discovered that appeasement was based on a fundamental misunderstanding of Hitler's aims: he was not going to be content with the union of all German-speakers. Hitler began to encourage the separatist feelings of the Slovaks. When the new Czech President, Hacha, was confronted with the demand that his country should be further divided up and that the Czech part of it should become part of the *Reich*, he gave in.

Key Term

Right of self-determination: the right of a racial group or population to decide its own future, normally used to mean the right of a group to unite with other people of the same race under a government of their choosing.

On 15 March, the Czech provinces of Bohemia and Moravia were occupied by German troops and became part of Germany. Slovakia was to be an independent state, though the Slovaks had to conduct their foreign policy along lines laid down by Berlin. A week later Hitler demanded that Lithuania hand back Memel, a city taken from Germany by the Versailles Treaty.

The Polish Crisis (1939)

After March 1939, it was obvious to Britain and France that the only way to stop Hitler was by fighting him.

31 March 1939 — Britain signed a treaty in which they promised to defend Poland if Poland was attacked. The Poles, encouraged by Britain's guarantee, decided to refuse Hitler's demand for Danzig and ordered partial military mobilisation.

April 1939 — Britain announced the introduction of conscription for 20-21 year olds. In order to undermine Britain's will to fight in defence of Poland, Hitler began by demanding just the return of Danzig, a mainly German-speaking city, and for rail and road access across the 'Polish Corridor' (separating East Prussia from the main part of Germany). Hitler ordered his generals to draw up plans for an attack on Poland.

April 1939 — Hitler secretly approached the Soviet Government for an alliance. This followed on lukewarm and ultimately abortive negotiations between the British and French on the one hand, and the USSR on the other, for collective military action to defend Poland.

The Nazi-Soviet Pact (August 1939)

This agreement, published on 23rd August 1939, came as a great shock to the British and French. Stalin was seeking to buy time in which to strengthen his armed forces for the war with Germany, which he believed to be inevitable.

The Pact also contained a secret agreement in which Russia and Germany divided up Poland between them and Russia was given permission to seize Estonia, Latvia and Lithuania and certain territories from Finland and Rumania.

Hitler may well have thought that the Pact would deter Britain and France from defending Poland. If it did not deter them, then the pact would ensure that a war between Germany and Poland did not escalate into a war between Germany and Russia.

Jan 1933 — Hitler appointed Chancellor

Sept 1933 — Germany left the Disarmament Conference and the League of Nations

July 1934 — Chancellor Dollfuss of Austria assassinated

Jan 1935 — Saar plebiscite

March 1935 — Conscription introduced;
Hitler announced that he would create an army of 550,000

April 1935 — The Stresa Front was signed by Britain, France and Italy

June 1935 — Anglo-German Naval Convention

Oct 1935 — Abyssinia invaded by Mussolini

March 1936 — Rhineland reoccupied by German troops

July 1936 — Spanish Civil War began

Oct 1936 — Rome-Berlin Axis signed

Nov 1936 — Anti-Comintern Pact signed by Germany and Japan

May 1937 — Bombing of Guernica by Luftwaffe in the Spanish Civil War

Nov 1937 — British Foreign Secretary Lord Halifax visited Berlin; Hossbach Memorandum

March 1938 — *Anschluss*–Austria united with Germany

12 Sept 1938 — Nuremberg rally—Hitler demanded the Sudetenland

15 Sept 1938 — Chamberlain visited Hitler at Berchtesgaden

18 Sept 1938	French Premier Daladier visited London
22 Sept 1938	Chamberlain met Hitler again at Bad Godesberg
29-30 Sept 1938	Munich Conference—Mussolini, Hitler, Daladier and Chamberlain agreed to hand the Sudetenland to Germany
Oct 1938	The Sudetenland was occupied by German troops
March 1939	Rest of Czechoslovakia occupied by Germany; Memel seized by Germany
May 1939	Pact of Steel—military alliance between Germany and Italy
Aug 1939	Nazi-Soviet Pact signed
1 Sept 1939	Poland invaded by Germany
3 Sept 1939	Britain and France declared war on Germany.

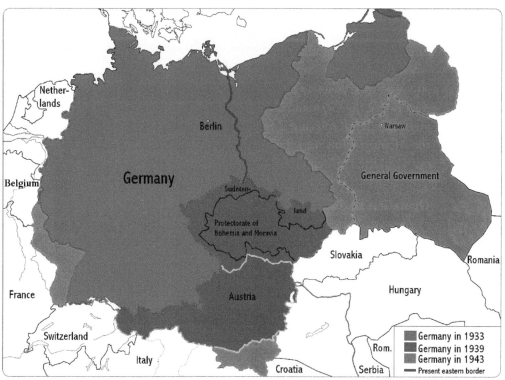

Figure 2.2: *Map showing Hitler's expansion of Germany*

2.5.3 The Outbreak of War in Europe

On 1st September 1939 Germany invaded Poland and, on 3rd September, Britain and France declared war on Germany. They were unable to offer any practical aid to the Poles, who were swiftly defeated by the Germans and by the Russians, who attacked Eastern Poland on 17th September. In October, the Poles surrendered. However, Britain and France refused to accept Germany's occupation of Poland and so Hitler was now committed to a major European war earlier than he had intended.

Blitzkrieg in the West

Hitler's main aim remained a war of conquest against the USSR and he therefore tried to get a negotiated peace with Britain and France in the autumn of 1939. When this failed, Hitler decided that before he attacked the Soviet Union he must achieve control over Western Europe.

In April 1940, German forces rapidly overran Denmark and Norway. On 10th May, German forces invaded Holland, Belgium, Luxembourg and France. By June, the first three countries had fallen and German troops were sweeping through France. The French surrendered on 22nd June. On 10 June, Mussolini decided to join in the war on Hitler's side and Italian troops invaded France.

The Battle of Britain

Hitler's spectacular victories were extremely popular in Germany but left Britain undefeated, although Britain had been forced to evacuate its expeditionary force at Dunkirk. Hitler still hoped for a negotiated peace but Churchill was defiant and Britain fought on. Hitler, therefore, decided that he must invade Britain in order to knock her out of the war before turning his attention to the USSR. However, the Luftwaffe failed to win control of the skies in the Battle of Britain.

Allies and Liabilities

It did not take Hitler long to discover that his ally, Mussolini, was more of a liability than an asset. Mussolini launched unsuccessful campaigns in the Balkans and North Africa and Hitler felt obliged to help Italy both in conquering Yugoslavia and Greece and in maintaining his position in North Africa. These campaigns delayed Hitler's invasion of the USSR until late June 1941, a delay that was arguably fatal to its success.

Meanwhile the German Navy, especially its U-boat (submarine) force, was given the job of starving Britain into surrender by sinking supply ships in the Atlantic. However, the campaign failed and Britain was able to hold out until the USA entered the war.

Operation Barbarossa

On 22nd June 1941, 3 million Axis troops invaded the USSR. Soviet forces, caught unprepared, retreated rapidly. By winter, the Germans were at the outskirts of Leningrad and were within 40 kilometres of Moscow, but the early onset of harsh winter conditions, for which they were ill equipped, and a brilliant counter-attack planned by Marshal Zhukov, using Russian troops transferred from the Far East, meant that Moscow did not fall. Hitler did not achieve the quick *blitzkrieg* victory he had hoped for. From 1942, the war in Russia became a long, drawn-out affair. The German economy was not geared to support this sort of warfare.

11 Dec 1941

Four days after the Japanese attack on Pearl Harbour, Hitler declared war on the USA, which had already been supplying Britain and Russia with vital war materials. Germany had now taken on two of the most powerful countries in the world.

1942

In many ways 1942 marked the point at which the pendulum of war began to swing against Germany. In October, in North Africa, the British, led by General Montgomery, scored a decisive victory at El Alamein. By May 1943, North Africa was fully under British and American control. In Russia, Hitler ordered an offensive southwards and eastwards towards the oil fields of Transcaucasia. This advance was held up at Stalingrad, which the Red Army defended heroically. Late in 1942, the Russians launched a great counter-offensive, trapping the German Sixth Army and forcing its surrender on 31 January 1943. Hitler could have withdrawn the Sixth Army from Stalingrad before it became encircled but he became obsessed with capturing the city that bore Stalin's name. About 100,000 Germans had died in the battle and 93,000 were taken prisoner. Stalingrad was a great material and psychological blow for the Germans, and showed how much Russian military leadership and capability had improved since 1941.

1943

In the summer of 1943 US and British forces invaded Sicily and Italy successfully. Mussolini was overthrown and his successor, Marshal Badoglio, surrendered to the British and Americans. However, German forces in Italy fought to delay the Allied advance up the peninsula, which was not completed until the spring of 1945. German commandos rescued Mussolini in September 1943 and Hitler set him up as puppet ruler of the Salo Republic. In April 1945, Mussolini was executed by Communist partisans.
On the Eastern Front in July 1943, the Red Army won a crushing victory at Kursk and began to drive the Germans westwards.

1944

In 1944 the Red Army drove the Germans completely out of the USSR and most of Eastern Europe as they advanced towards Berlin. In the West, Britain and America launched the largest amphibious invasion in history on the Normandy coast on D-Day, 6 June 1944. Paris was liberated in August, and, by the autumn, Allied troops had reached the Rhine. Hitler's last offensive in the West, the 'Battle of the Bulge' of December 1944–January 1945, temporarily pushed the Allies back but failed to alter the course of the war.

1945

In February 1945, Russian troops invaded Germany and, in the West, the British and Americans had crossed the Rhine and were advancing on Berlin. By late April, Berlin was besieged by the Red Army. On 30 April, Hitler committed suicide in his bunker in the grounds of the Chancellery in Berlin. In May, Germany surrendered. Goering and other leading Nazis were captured, stood trial at Nuremburg and were sentenced to death or to terms of imprisonment for the war crimes they had committed. 4.5 million Germans had been killed in the war and almost six million of Europe's Jews had died in the Holocaust.

Figure 2.3: *Hitler at the Kroll Opera House declaring war on the USA, 11 December, 1941*

Key Historical Perspectives: How appropriate is the term 'totalitarian' as a description of the Third *Reich*?

Carl Friedrich and Zbigniew Brzezinski in their study Totalitarian Dictatorship and Autocracy (Harvard, 1956) identified the following characteristics of a totalitarian state:

1. Single party dictatorship.
2. Cult of the leader.
3. *"An elaborate ideology, consisting of an official body of doctrine covering all vital aspects of man's existence to which everyone living in that society is supposed to adhere".*
4. A system of terror…effected through party and secret-police control'.
5. A monopoly of control by the party and the government of the media and all cultural activity.
6. Control of all aspects of citizens' lives through propaganda, education, mass organisations.
7. Centralised control and direction of the entire economy.

The Third *Reich* displayed many of these characteristics. However, it is evident that there were definite limits to totalitarianism in Nazi Germany. This is, at least to a considerable extent, because the Third *Reich* only survived for twelve years. Many historians since the 1980s, such as Hans Mommsen and Robert Gellately, have questioned how far Nazi controls really extended. Gellately suggests that Nazi terror relied on relatively small numbers of Gestapo officers and a considerable degree of collusion by ordinary Germans in informing on each other.

Key Historical Perspectives: Was Hitler a 'Weak' or 'Strong' dictator?

Historians have argued about whether Hitler was a 'strong' (e.g. Alan Bullock) or 'weak' (e.g. Martin Broszat) dictator.

Certainly, Hitler undermined orderly government in Germany:

- He had a habit of appointing several people to practically the same job, resulting in officials competing for Hitler's favour ('working towards the Führer')

- He added to existing institutions rather than destroying them; he created Supreme Reich Authorities whose functions often overlapped with existing ministries, e.g. the Four-Year Plan office (under Goering) overlapped with the Todt Organisation (road and defence building) and with the Economics Ministry.

- Hitler destroyed cabinet or collective government in Germany; the Cabinet met seventy-two times in 1933, nineteen times in 1934, four times in 1936 and not at all after 1938.

- Although Hitler was in a good position to co-ordinate policy as the single source of authority in Germany, he failed to do so because he became increasingly lazy and was not interested in day-to-day government business, particularly in domestic policy.

Whether or not the resulting chaos was deliberate (the result of Hitler playing off ministers against each other) or unintended (the result of the 'legal revolution' of 1933/1934), it did not prevent Hitler from pursuing his main goals of territorial expansion and the creation of a 'pure' race.

3. AIMS AND RESULTS OF NAZI POLICIES

TOPICS:
Long-term conditions
Short-term conditions
Methods

3.1 Nazi Ideology

> **Key Historical Perspectives:** Was Nazism a distinct ideology?
>
> National Socialism developed many of the forms of an ideology. However, historians such as Martin Broszat have argued that Nazism lacked a distinct ideology and view Nazism as merely a branch of **Fascism**, sharing a Europe-wide militarism, hatred of communism and stressing centralism within the state.
>
> Other historians (Hugh Trevor-Roper, Alan Bullock), whilst accepting that Nazi ideology was not clearly defined, argue that the 'Führer principle' was of particular importance to German fascism and, above all, stress that Hitler provided Nazism (see *Mein Kampf*) with a unique racial and **anti-semitic** programme, which was absent in Italian fascism. Yet the Nazis' Twenty-Five Points of 1920 were a curious mixture of nationalist and socialist elements. It soon became clear that Hitler was not particularly committed to the socialist element.

🔑 Key Term

Fascism: extreme nationalist and authoritarian movement that emerged in interwar Europe and became particularly prominent in Germany and Italy.

🔑 Key Term

Anti-semitic: anti-Jewish.

3.2 Social Policies

1. Treatment of Minorities

In Hitler's eyes, the *volk* community was everything, the individual nothing. Hitler aimed to create a society in which every individual saw the purpose of their life as contributing to the greater good of the German *volk* (people); Hitler attacked the idea of individual rights as damaging to the national community. Hitler believed that his 'people community'—*Volksgemeinschaft*—would be superior to all others, composed of pure Aryan Germans. There would be no room for '**asocials**', the disabled, or non-Aryans in Hitler's Germany.

i. Nazi Policy Towards Asocials

- In 1936 an 'asocial colony' Hashude was set up for those groups whose lifestyles did not conform to Nazi expectations, e.g. chronic alcoholics. Initially the idea was to re-educate them, so that they could become socially useful citizens but in the late 1930s many were sent to concentration camps.

🔑 Key Term

Asocials: people hostile to or refusing to conform to social norms; the Nazis labelled groups such as alcoholics, beggars and prostitutes 'asocials'.

- The Nazis also targeted homosexuals on the grounds that they allegedly engaged in 'unnatural behaviour' – Himmler set up the *Reich* Central Office for the Combatting of Homosexuality in 1936. From the late 1930s, many homosexuals were sent to concentration camps, castrated or executed.

- About 10,000 tramps were sent to concentration camps and many died in them.

ii. Nazi Policy Towards the Disabled

> **Key Term**
>
> **Eugenics:** a movement that was influential in a number of European countries and the USA in the first decades of the 20th Century that aimed to improve the genetic quality of a race, for example, by sterilising people who have disabilities in an attempt to eliminate defective genes from the racial gene pool.

Eugenics had been increasingly influential in the 1920s in Germany and elsewhere; in 1932 the Prussian Health Council had proposed voluntary sterilisation for certain hereditary illnesses. In July 1933, the Law for the Prevention of the Hereditarily Diseased Progeny made it compulsory for people with a wide range of hereditary illnesses to be sterilised, such as those with hereditary blindness and schizophrenia. Some of these illnesses were, in fact, not hereditary, for example, alcoholism. 320,000 people were sterilised.

1939–1941 saw the Nazis pursue a euthanasia programme against the physically and mentally handicapped. 72,000 were killed. The Nazis tried but failed to keep it secret and a number of people protested, notably Cardinal von Galen.

iii. The Nazis' Racial Policies

The Nazis aimed to prevent members of 'inferior' races from 'polluting' the *Volksgemeinschaft*. The Nazi classified the Sinti and Roma (more commonly referred to as 'gypsies'), Slavs and Jews as 'inferior' races.

a. Treatment of the Sinti and Roma (gypsy communities)

The Nazis were hostile to gypsies because they were often of 'mixed race' and itinerant, so came frequently into contact with 'Aryan' Germans, with the risk of 'Aryan' blood being 'contaminated' by resultant sexual relations. In 1936 the Nazis set up a Reich Central Office for the Fight Against the Gypsy Nuisance.

From 1939, gypsies were forced to live in specially assigned sites and from 1942 became victims of the Final Solution, alongside the Jews and other 'inferior races'. 25,000 out of Germany's 30,000 gypsies died in camps during the Second World War, most of them at Auschwitz.

b. Anti-Semitic Policies

The Jews were singled out by Hitler in *Mein Kampf* as the greatest threat to the Aryan race. Once in power, Nazi policy towards the Jews developed in a number of stages and historians are divided over whether Hitler had from the early 1930s onwards the aim of exterminating the Jewish race or whether the Nazis' anti-semitic policies developed in a more haphazard fashion.

 April 1933 The SA organised a one-day boycott of Jewish businesses. As a result of the passing of the Law for the Restoration of a Professional Civil Service, Jewish civil servants were sacked.

 Nov 1935 The Nuremberg Laws deprived Jews of German citizenship and forbade marriage and sexual relations between Jews and Aryan Germans.

 Nov 1938 *Kristallnacht*, a series of violent attacks on Jews and Jewish properties and synagogues, was launched by the Nazis – 20,000 Jews were sent to the camps. Following this, Jewish doctors and lawyers were forbidden to work for Aryans and Jewish children had to be taught in separate schools.

1939-1941 Increasing restrictions were imposed on Germany's Jewish community, including obliging Jews to wear the Star of David to identify themselves and being forced to move into ghettoes.

1942 At the Wannsee Conference, leading Nazis decided on the Final Solution: the extermination of Jews, which saw 6 million die in death camps such as Auschwitz, Treblinka and Sobibor.

> **Key Historical Perspectives:** German anti-semitism
>
> The historian Daniel Goldhagen *(Hitler's Willing Executioners)* has sparked a great controversy by arguing that the German people were, and had been for centuries, virulently and uniquely anti-semitic and that ordinary Germans did not just stand by whilst the Jews were persecuted but took pleasure in attacking the Jews, including their murder in the Second World War.
>
> Many historians (particularly Ruth Bettina Birn) have criticised Goldhagen for selective use of evidence and argue that Germans pre-1933 had not been particularly anti-semitic. Omer Bartov, among many other academics, has raised doubts about Goldhagen's research, pointing out that Goldhagen's thesis is based on a study of only those Germans who served as policemen during World War II, a narrow cross section of the population. The fact that, in 1933, Hitler turned down demands from the SA for more than a one day boycott of Jewish shops for fear of a hostile response both inside and outside Germany suggests that Hitler doubted that anti-semitism had wide support among Germans.

The evidence suggests that though many Germans had a generalised dislike of Jews they got on well with their Jewish neighbours and failed to respond to Nazi propaganda aimed at inciting hatred of the Jews.

2. Policies Towards Women

Hitler's ideas about women were very traditional. He believed that the woman's place was in the home, doing the housework, cooking meals, bearing and rearing children and being obedient to her husband. The Nazi slogan *Kinder, Kirche und Kuche* (Children, Church, Kitchen), defined the spheres of activity to which the Nazis wanted to confine women. Women were encouraged to wear modest clothes and little or no make-up.

The number of places for female students in universities was reduced and women found jobs harder to get. The girls' section of the Nazi Youth Movement encouraged girls to see their future as a domestic one, and the Nazi Women's Movement, headed by Gertrude Scholz-Klink, trained adult women in housewifely skills such as embroidery. Scholz-Klink proclaimed that, *"The German woman is knitting again!"*

Hitler's Address to the Nazi Women's League in 1934:

"The slogan 'Emancipation of women' was invented by Jewish intellectuals and its content was formed by the same spirit. In the really good times of German life the German woman had no need to emancipate herself ... We do not consider it right for the woman to interfere in the world of the man ... Every child that a woman brings into the world is a battle, a battle waged for the existence of her people... The programme of our National Socialist Women's movement has in reality but one single point, and that point is the child, that tiny creature which must be born and grow strong and which alone gives meaning to the whole life struggle."

The Nazis took Weimar policies to restrict female employment much further:

- Married women were often excluded from the civil service and other professions.
- Restrictions were placed on the number of women at university. From 1933, women who left work to marry (an Aryan) received an interest free marriage loan; the amount to be repaid fell by 25% with each child born.
- The Women's Enterprise (DFW) organised training in domestic skills; by 1939, 3.5 million women had attended courses.

The Nazis were very anxious to increase the birth-rate; it had been falling across Europe in the 1920s but most severely in Germany and this had potentially serious consequences for the Nazis' expansionist aims.

In the 1930s the Nazis tried a number of policies to increase the birth-rate, including awarding medals for prolific mothers: bronze for four to five children, silver for six to seven and gold for eight or more. Women were encouraged to lead healthy lifestyles and divorce was made easier for those in childless marriages.

The birth-rate did rise from 990,000 in 1932 to 1.28 million in 1937, but this was well short of the 1.6 million births of 1920 and probably was more the result of improved economic conditions.

However, from 1936 the Nazis had to modify their employment policies because of labour shortages and growing numbers of women were recruited into factories and businesses. By 1939 more women were in employment than in 1933, and, by 1943, women were conscripted into war work.

3. Policy Towards Young People

i. Nazi Youth Movements

Young people were of particular importance to the Nazis as they were Germany's future and were also more susceptible to indoctrination. The Hitler Youth (Hitler *Jugend*) was set up 1925; in 1933 there were only 55,000 members, whereas total youth groups in Germany numbered 5 to 6 million members.

April 1933 — All other youth groups, except for those run by the Catholic Church, were closed down and absorbed into the Hitler Youth (HJ).

Nov 1935 — All youth groups were incorporated into the HJ. By 1939, 82% of all 11–18 year olds were in the HJ or League of German Maidens (the equivalent for girls).

Nov 1938 — Membership of the Hitler Youth became compulsory.

Boys were trained for war, women for motherhood. The HJ became less popular in the late 1930s as activities and discipline became more militarised and membership became compulsory. Alternative youth groups, illegal after 1936, attracted growing numbers.

Anti-HJ groups:

- The Edelweiss Pirates: they included a number of regional groups, e.g. the Navajos of Cologne, and were predominantly working class. They refused to join the HJ. They organised their own activities and often beat up HJ members. They were rarely involved in political activities but a few joined resistance groups in the war. The Nazis found them difficult to deal with, partly because there was no organised leadership that they could target. In 1944 the Nazis did hang the leaders of the Cologne Pirates.

- The Swing Movement: these were middle/upper class youth groups who rejected the HJ. They, unlike the Edelweiss pirates, did not meet in parks or on the streets but tended to do so in night clubs or their parents' homes; they angered the Nazis by dancing to American, black music and wearing English style clothing. These alternative groups reveal the limit to Nazi controls.

ii. Education

The main aim of Nazi educational policy was to develop loyalty to the regime; there was no emphasis on developing the individual's abilities.

In 1933 the Law for Restoration of a Professional Civil Service led to a purge of teachers; by 1937 the Nazi Teachers' League represented 97% of all teachers.

Lessons, particularly History and Biology, became politicised; there was a much greater emphasis on Physical Education in schools and eugenics was introduced. Teachers increasingly became disillusioned because of constant Party interference and as a result of being undermined by the HJ.

4. Policies Towards the Churches

Though Nazi propaganda made frequent references to God, the Nazi leaders privately despised Christianity, which they saw as a religion of love and charity which made people soft. Himmler certainly looked forward to the victory of National Socialism over Christianity. Nevertheless, the Christian churches in Germany were strong and Hitler knew that a confrontation with them would be dangerous. He played down the anti-Christian element in Nazi thought and tried to keep on good terms with Church leaders while at the same time attempting to bring the churches under government supervision.

a. The Catholic Church

The Nazis lacked the confidence to destroy the established churches though they did undermine them. In the case of the Catholic Church, Hitler signed an agreement, the Concordat, with the Pope in 1933, under which Catholic bishops had to take an oath of loyalty to the Nazi state.

In 1936 the Nazis broke the Concordat by closing down Catholic youth organisations and by beginning to close monasteries. This led to the Pope denouncing the Nazi regime in his 1937 encyclical *With Burning Concern*.

In 1941 the Catholic press was closed down. However, the Church survived and some individual Catholic clergy spoke out against the Nazis, particularly Cardinal Galen who in 1941 denounced the murder of the handicapped; his sermon was printed and widely distributed.

b. The Protestant Churches

The Nazis tried a different strategy with the Protestant Church, trying to infiltrate it and control it from within. Some Protestants, the German Christians, wanted to create a new version of Christianity in which Jesus would be presented as an Aryan rather than a Jew and the Old Testament would be banned.

Hitler tried to make one of the German Christians, Pastor Müller, the head of a united Protestant Church but the scheme failed because many Protestants rejected Müller's ideas. Although the German Christians won 75% of the votes in church elections in 1933 and their leader, Ludwig Muller, was made Reich Bishop, the following year dissenting clergy set up the 'Confessional Church' in opposition to Nazi attempts to Nazify the Church. Pastor Niemoller led the Confessional Clergy and a majority of clergy joined them. Niemoller was imprisoned in 1938.

Therefore, the Churches to some extent continued to provide sources of values and information different from the Nazi regime.

3.3 Economic Policies

When Hitler became Chancellor in January 1933, he knew that his continuing popularity depended on his being able to tackle Germany's economic problems, particularly unemployment, successfully.

At the same time, he was determined to rearm Germany and to prepare for war. For both these reasons he wanted to rebuild the German economy.

Hitler needed the support of industrialists and so used Hjalmar Schacht as Reichsbank President and Reich Economics Minister (1934–1937). Hitler ignored the socialist elements in the Nazis' Twenty-Five Points and rejected SA calls for nationalisation of big businesses in a 'second revolution'. Many industrialists became very closely identified with the regime, e.g. Krupp (steel/arms manufacturer) and IG Farben (chemicals).

Hitler had no coherent economic plan in January 1933; he adopted three approaches:

3. Autarky: economic self-sufficiency

4. Deficit financing: spending money on job creation, large-scale borrowing

5. *Wehrwirtschaft:* an economy geared to the demands of war.

Until 1936 Hitler followed fairly orthodox financial policies – the New Plan (September 1934) involved government control of foreign exchange and bilateral trade agreements, particularly with south-east European countries. Peasant farmers were protected by tariffs on imported food, and helped by cheap loans and tax exemptions.

Hitler addressed the problem of high unemployment by a variety of methods. He was aided by the fact that, by 1933, world trade was starting to recover and unemployment had peaked by late 1932, but nonetheless his success in creating new jobs and reviving industry was substantial:

Year	Numbers of Unemployed in Germany (in millions)
1932 (December)	5.6
1934	2.3
1937	0.9
1938	0.2

How did the Nazis bring down unemployment?

- They spent money on public works programmes, schemes to build new houses, plant forests and reclaim land. Total government spending rose from RM 8.6 billion in 1932 to RM 29.3 billion by 1938.
- They encouraged the expansion of the car industry by removing the luxury tax on cars, cutting the tax on petrol and beginning a programme of *autobahn* building which gave Germany a new motorway network.
- They offered cash incentives to persuade women to give up their jobs.
- After 1935, they instituted a massive re-armament programme created hundreds of thousands of new jobs in industry.
- They reintroduced conscription in 1935. This helped to bring unemployment down by taking young men between the ages of 18 and 20 out of the job market.

By 1937 there was a shortage of skilled labour. All this government spending helped stimulate economic growth and restored confidence.

Industrial Output

In 1933 industrial production was only 66% of its pre-Depression level, but by 1937 Germany was producing more than she had in the most prosperous Weimar years.

Germany's Gross National Product (GNP)

Key Term

Gross National Product: total value of goods and services provided by a country.

Year	GNP in billions of *Reichsmark*
1928	72
1933	44
1938	80

Wage Levels

Wages recovered considerably: in 1933, average wages in Germany were only 77% of their 1928 level but by 1939 they were 89% of the 1928 level. Overall, German workers benefitted from falling unemployment and rising wages but, in real terms, wages were not quite as high as in the best years of Weimar.

The Four-Year Plan (1936)

Hitler's achievements in tackling unemployment and stimulating economic growth were offset by a serious problem. To rearm Germany Hitler needed to import more fuel and raw materials such as rubber, bauxite and iron ore. This worsened Germany's balance of payment problem (Germany was importing much more than it was exporting).

By the end of 1935, Hitler's advisers told him that Germany could not afford both to import all the food she was importing and to import all the industrial raw materials. This is often referred to as the 'Guns or Butter?' crisis. Hitler felt that he could not risk cutting down on the availability of food because this might make his government unpopular, so he decided instead to try to make Germany self-sufficient in industrial raw materials.

Goering was put in charge of the Four-Year Plan, which began in 1936. The plan was intended to make synthetic substitutes for imported oil and rubber and to devise ways of using Germany's poor quality coal and iron ore. This marked a departure from traditional economic policy and was opposed by Hjalmar Schacht, Hitler's Economics Minister, who resigned in 1937.

Hitler, in a secret 'Four-Year Plan Memorandum', outlined the need to gear the economy for war within four years. Overall, the Plan was not a success. The scheme to produce artificial rubber ('BUNA') worked, and production of synthetic fuel doubled, but in most other categories of production, targets were not met.

By the time the war broke out Germany was still dependent on imported fuel and raw materials, particularly on iron ore from Sweden. Furthermore, the subsidising of inefficient small peasant farmers by the Nazi regime meant that by 1939 Germany was still importing 19% of its food requirements.

Gearing the Economy for War: Rearmament

Year	Government spending on armaments in billions of *Reichsmark*
1932	0.8
1933	1.9
1935	6.0
1938	17.2

- In 1933 Germany had an army of 100,000 men, no tanks, no warplanes and a navy of limited tonnage.
- By 1939 the Germans had 1,200 bombers and ninety-eight divisions in their Army, though about a third of these were untrained and disorganised. The Navy comprised two battleships, two armoured cruisers, seventeen destroyers and forty-seven U-boats.

The period 1936–1939 saw a massive increase in arms spending; 66% of German industrial investment was devoted to war production.

Despite this huge increase in armaments expenditure, Germany would not be ready for total war (the total mobilisation of the economy to support a long war) until the mid-1940s.

Key Historical Perspectives: Was Hitler preparing for total or limited war?

Historians are divided over whether Hitler had planned to get Germany prepared for total war prior to 1939. Some historians argue that Hitler never intended to achieve full mobilisation of the economy because he aimed to wage a series of short, *blitzkrieg* campaigns, which would allow Germany to exploit the economic resources of conquered countries before launching another attack. According to this interpretation, Hitler's strategy failed when he became trapped in a long war of attrition with the USSR from June 1941, which ultimately led to the USSR (and its allies) wearing Germany down.

However, other historians, notably Richard Overy, suggest that Hitler was planning for total war rather than *blitzkrieg* campaigns, but miscalculated in 1939 as he did not think his invasion of Poland would provoke a general European war.

Key Historical Perspectives: Was Hitler forced by a growing economic crisis to go to war in 1939?

Tim Mason has argued that growing inflationary pressures – Schacht's resignation as President of the *Reichsbank* in January 1939 was partly because of economic concerns – and increasing working-class discontent with the limited supply of consumer goods (consumer good production rose by 69% in the period 1933–1938 compared to a 389% increase in industrial goods over the same period), and the failure of wages in the late 1930s to rise in real terms, shaped Hitler's decision to go to war in 1939. Mason suggests that Hitler was seeking to escape from these growing economic problems by going to war.

However, most historians have rejected Mason's thesis. Mason's critics argue that firstly, growing economic difficulties did not amount to a crisis and, secondly, that it was diplomatic and military considerations, rather than economic factors, which influenced Hitler's decision over the timing of war.

Essay Writing Activities on the Rise and Rule of the Nazi Authoritarian State

Below you will find two essay questions, which cover most of the issues that I have dealt with in this guide. By examining these questions, you will be able to test your understanding and recall of the material and, in addition, practise your essay writing skills. I have given you some ideas about how they could be tackled and then provided you with space to add examples and further points.

Practice Essay Question 1

Examine how any one leader you have studied exploited conditions to create an authoritarian state.

Firstly, you need to take the question apart and see that you are being asked to examine both the conditions which prevailed in the Weimar Republic which made possible Hitler's creation of a Nazi regime and the methods he used to take advantage of those conditions. Secondly, you should see that the question requires you to consider developments up to July 1933 (rather than just January 1933, when Hitler became chancellor) when the Nazi Party became the sole legal party.

In terms of examining 'conditions' which gave rise to the Third Reich, you might either group these into short (1929–1933) and long-term (since 1918) or, alternatively, adopt a thematic approach (probably better, less likely to lead you into a narrative which becomes unfocussed) in which you look at 'political', 'economic' and 'social' conditions. In order to write a really good answer, you should look to establish links between these conditions. With reference to the methods by which Hitler exploited these conditions, you need to ensure that you link methods to conditions, rather than simply describing what Hitler's methods were.

Below this paragraph, you will see some points relating to different types of conditions, which played a part in the creation of a single party state in Germany. I have left space so you can add more points and examples to illustrate the key points.

Political conditions

Long-term

- The Republic was handicapped because of its association with the hated Versailles Treaty. Nationalist hostility towards the Republic was shown by the Kapp *Putsch* (1920).
- The Weimar constitution contained weaknesses; proportional representation, given the existence of a large number of parties, made for a series of short-lived coalition governments. The constitution also gave the President enormous power, particularly through Article 48.

Other long-term political conditions:

_____

_____

_____

(continued)

Political conditions *(continued)*

Short-term

- Collapse of the 'Grand Coalition' in 1930 after the SPD walked out because of an argument with the Centre over cutting unemployment benefit.
- Growing political polarisation in 1930–1933, saw the rise of both the NSDAP and the KPD (the latter gained 17% of the votes cast in Nov 1932 elections).
- The *Reichstag* Fire (February 1933) increased the propertied classes' fear of a communist revolution.

Other short-term political conditions:

Economic conditions

- Early economic crisis 1919–1923; many of the middle class were permanently alienated by a loss of savings during the hyper-inflation.
- Germany was hit particularly hard by the effects of the Wall Street Crash (1929), causing soaring unemployment.

More points about economic conditions:

How was Hitler able to exploit the above conditions?

- Hitler—charismatic leadership, oratory
- Hitler saw after the Munich *Putsch* (1923) that the way to power had to be by means of 'legal revolution'. Hitler committed the NSDAP to becoming the largest party in the *Reichstag*.
- By forming an alliance with Hugenberg and the DNVP from 1929
- As a result of the *Reichstag* Fire, Hitler was able to persuade Hindenburg to declare a state of emergency
- The Enabling Act (March 1933) gave Hitler the power to make law without the *Reichstag*; he used this power to dismantle democracy and create a single party state.

Other points about how Hitler was able to exploit conditions:

Conclusion

Practice Essay Question 2

To what extent were the social and economic policies of any one 20th century authoritarian state you have studied successful?

In answering this question, first it is necessary to identify what the Nazis' aims were. Below I have started by pointing to the debate among historians about the nature of the Nazis' aims and then listing their main aims. Following this, I have created a detailed plan which examines the Nazis' success in certain areas of policy. I have also just indicated certain other aims that would merit assessment in this essay and I have left space for you to provide your own points and examples/evidence you might use in answering this question. Under 'social policy' you could consider other areas such as Nazi policies towards women and Germany's youth.

The historiographical debate

Was Hitler an 'intentionalist' (according to Bullock, Trevor-Roper) with a set agenda or was the Nazi regime opportunist/functionalist (according to Broszat, Mommsen) which lacked clearly formulated aims and instead responded to circumstances in a chaotic fashion (Hitler as 'weak dictator')?

How do we know what the Nazis' aims were? – The Twenty-Five Points (1920), *Mein Kampf* (1925), Four-Year Plan Memorandum (1936), Hossbach Memorandum (1937).

The Nazis were not united, especially over the socialist elements of the Twenty-Five Point programme; Gregor Strasser and many of the SA leaders sought a 'second revolution' involving the creation of a people's army and the nationalisation of big businesses. By 1933, Hitler had rejected these demands.

What were the Nazis' aims in social and economic policy?

1. Economic: to revive the German economy in order to (a) maintain domestic support by reducing unemployment, (b) to support rearmament achieve *autarky*.

2. 'Gleichschaltung': to create a totalitarian state in which all aspects of Germans' lives were 'co-ordinated'– controlled and indoctrinated in line with Nazi ideology.

3. To create a master race.

How successful were these aims?

1. In Economic policy?

- Mopped up unemployment very successfully (only 0.2 million by 1938) by means of deficit financing, public works schemes, rearmament
- Industrial output reached record levels; by 1939 GNP was 33% higher than in 1929
- Huge rearmament—66% of investment went on rearmament in the period 1936–1939.

But there were limits to this success and serious problems emerged:

- Nazi officials and economics experts/businessmen were divided over the 'Guns or Butter Crisis' in 1936. Hitler responded with the Four-Year Plan.
- The economy was not geared for total war by the end of 1939 (some historians question whether this was Hitler's aim, Richard Overy argues that it was).
- 1939–1941 saw a huge increase in investment in rearmament but this was inefficiently managed. Only under Albert Speer (from 1942) was there efficient co-ordination of war production. He trebled weapons production in two years.
- Inflationary pressures began to build from 1937, this was partly why Schacht resigned as Economics Minister. Tim Mason argued that Hitler went to war in 1939 in order to escape a growing economic crisis; however, this view is not generally shared by historians.
- Autarky failed; Germany was still dependent on imports, particularly food (importing 19% of its requirements in 1939) and Swedish iron ore.

(continued)

- Real wages in the late 1930s were below the 1928 level and consumer good production lagged far behind that of industrial goods; this reflects Hitler's priorities (i.e. rearmament paramount after 1936).

2. In creating a totalitarian society?

_____

_____

_____

_____

_____

3. In creating a master race?

_____

_____

_____

_____

_____

_____

Conclusion:

_____

_____

_____

_____

_____

Image Credits

Figure 1.1 *American cartoon from New York World (1921) suggesting that reparations were an unreasonable burden on Germany.*
Source: Current History, Volume 13, New York Times Company, 1921 [public domain], via Wikimedia Commons (File uploaded by user: Guest2625)

Figure 2.1 *Prisoners barracks at Dachau Concentration Camp.*
Source: U.S. Holocaust Museum, photograph #37255 [public domain], via Wikimedia Commons (File uploaded by user: Hohum)

Figure 2.2 *Map showing Hitler's expansion of Germany.*
Source: Author: Wikinist [CC BY-SA 3.0 (http://creativecommons.org/licenses/by-sa/3.0/)], via Wikimedia Commons

Figure 2.3 *Hitler at the Kroll Opera House declaring war on the USA, 11 December, 1941.*
Source: Unknown photographer, German Federal Archives, Accession number: Bild 183-1987-0703-507 [CC BY-SA 3.0 (http://creativecommons.org/licenses/by-sa/3.0/)], via Wikimedia Commons (File uploaded by user: Owain Knight)

IBDP REVISION COURSES

Summary

Who are they for?
Students about to take their final
IBDP exams (May or November)

Locations include:
Oxford, UK
Rome, Italy
Brussels, Belgium
Dubai, UAE
Adelaide, Sydney & Melbourne, AUS
Munich, Germany

Duration
2.5 days per subject
Students can take multiple subjects

The most successful IB revision courses worldwide

Highly-experienced IB teachers and examiners

Every class is tailored to the needs of that particular group of students

Features

- Classes grouped by grade (UK)
- Exam skills and techniques – typical traps identified
- Exam practice
- Pre-course online questionnaire to identify problem areas
- Small groups of 8–10 students
- 24-hour pastoral care.

Revising for the final IB exams without expert guidance is tough. Students attending OSC Revision Courses get more work done in a shorter time than they could possibly have imagined.

With a different teacher, who is confident in their subject and uses their experience and expertise to explain new approaches and exam techniques, students rapidly improve their understanding. OSC's teaching team consists of examiners and teachers with years of experience – they have the knowledge and skills students need to get top grades.

The size of our Oxford course gives some particular advantages to students. With over 1,000 students and 300 classes, we can group students by grade – enabling them to go at a pace that suits them.

Students work hard, make friends and leave OSC feeling invigorated and confident about their final exams.

We understand the needs of IBDP students – our decades of experience, hand-picked teachers and intense atmosphere can improve your grades.

> "I got 40 points overall, two points up from my prediction of 38, and up 7 points from what I had been scoring in my mocks over the years, before coming to OSC. Thank you so much for all your help!"
>
> OSC Student

Please note that locations and course features are subject to change - please check our website for up-to-date details.

Find out more: ⌂ osc-ib.com/revision 📱 +44 (0)1865 512802

MID IBDP SUMMER PROGRAMMES

Summary

Who is it for?
For students entering their final year of the IB Diploma Programme

Locations include:
Harvard and MIT, USA
Cambridge, UK

Duration
Min. 1 week, max. 6 weeks
1 or 2 IB subjects per week

- Improve confidence and grades
- Highly-experienced IB teachers and examiners
- Tailored classes to meet students' needs
- Wide range of available subjects
- Safe accommodation and 24-hour pastoral care

Features

- Morning teaching in chosen IB subject
- 2nd IB subject afternoon classes
- IB Skills afternoon classes
- One-to-one Extended Essay Advice, Private Tuition and University Guidance options
- Small classes
- Daily homework
- Unique IB university fair
- Class reports for parents
- Full social programme.

By the end of their first year, students understand the stimulating and challenging nature of the IB Diploma.

They also know that the second year is crucial in securing the required grades to get into their dream college or university.

This course helps students to avoid a 'summer dip' by using their time effectively. With highly-experienced IB teachers, we consolidate a student's year one learning, close knowledge gaps, and introduce some year two material.

In a relaxed environment, students develop academically through practice revision and review. They are taught new skills, techniques, and perspectives – giving a real boost to their grades. This gives students an enormous amount of confidence and drive for their second year.

The whole experience was incredible. The university setting was inspiring, the friends I made, and the teaching was first-class. I feel so much more confident in myself and in my subject.

OSC Student

Please note that locations and course features are subject to change - please check our website for up-to-date details.

Find out more: osc-ib.com/mid +44 (0)1865 512802